Research report 35

ARTS COUNCIL ENGLAND

The art of inclusion

Helen Jermyn

Contents

List of tables

Foreword and acknowledgements

In 1999, the UK Government Social Exclusion Unit reported through Policy Action Team (PAT) 10 on the role of the arts and sport on neighbourhood renewal. A key finding of PAT 10 was that participation in arts and sports could support community development through impacting on the indicators of health, crime, education and employment. On the arts side there was little evidence to support this claim and PAT 10 recommended that funding bodies should 'wherever possible make external evaluation and the means to carry it out integral to the funded project/programme and ensure that the criteria against which success will be judged are clearly established and derived directly from the expressed needs and aims of those participating' (DCMS, 1999).

Arts Council England's response to PAT 10, *Addressing social exclusion: a framework for action* (ACE, 2000), included a programme of evaluation of arts projects with social inclusion aims as part of the New Audiences Programme. Two researchers, Helen Jermyn and Gerri Moriarty, worked on the evaluation programme; Helen completed a literature review in 2001, Gerri's review of how evaluation can be used by small/mid-scale arts companies and projects to support their work, *Sharing our practice*, was completed in 2002; and now in 2004 we have the third and final in-depth report by Helen.

This report is based on an analysis of three broad models of arts intervention – community-led work; experienced arts organisations working with socially excluded groups; and experienced arts organisations working alongside less experienced, usually much larger, arts organisations to share their skills in this area. Helen's task was not an easy one and her report clearly illustrates the many challenges facing those seeking to evaluate the impact of the arts using an objective and rational process. The report illustrates that the high-level outcomes desired by some stakeholders regarding direct impacts on health, crime, education, employment etc are largely unrealistic when applied to short-term projects. Participants do cite many positive benefits to participation in arts projects but these are largely of a personal and transitory nature. As well as supporting rigorous research on the impact of the arts, as arts funders, we perhaps also need to be more robust in valuing individual testimony and in encouraging the process of participation and engagement in the arts as an end in itself.

Only in-depth longitudinal studies with established organisations or projects will provide evidence of the unique long-term contribution the arts make in achieving broader social and economic outcomes.

Arts Council England would like to thank Helen and all those individuals and organisations who worked on the analysis and evaluation of their projects. Our thanks also to the members of the Social Inclusion Steering Group who have supported Arts Council England's work on this project throughout the last three years.

Aileen McEvoy
Director of External Relations, Arts Council England, North West

Executive summary

Introduction

In January 2001, the former Arts Council of England and Regional Arts Boards commissioned research to explore social inclusion work in the arts. The overall objectives of the research were to:

- gather evidence that could be used to inform policy and advocacy initiatives
- develop and test appropriate methodologies for evaluating arts initiatives with aims related to social inclusion
- evaluate three different models of initiating and delivering projects
- identify the characteristics of successful initiatives and approaches that did not work and the reasons for this
- develop measures of success that could be used to evaluate a broad range of initiatives

The research comprised two independent, but related, strands of work:

- a self-evaluation strand, conducted by arts consultant Gerri Moriarty, involved working with arts organisations to help them evaluate their own practice and producing an evaluation guide for arts organisations undertaking work in the area of social exclusion. The resulting report, *Sharing Practice*, was published in 2002
- an external evaluation strand, conducted by independent researcher Helen Jermyn, explored practice and outcomes. This report presents the key findings from this second research strand

Methodology

Sampling

Twenty-eight arts organisations participated in the research. Initially, this sample was made up of organisations the Arts Council had selected as exemplars of good practice in the area of social inclusion work. At a later stage, additional projects funded through the Social Inclusion strand of the New Audiences Programme were added to the sample. Fifteen projects, nine of which were New Audience projects, were developed into case studies. Most of the projects were participatory arts projects with a wide range of arts and crafts represented, including digital arts, textiles, painting, mural-making, photography, writing, music-making and drama. Participating groups ranged from older people living in sheltered accommodation to families with children aged under 5, and projects took place in settings ranging from prisons to theatres, from community centres to hostels for the homeless.

The research set out to explore three different models of social inclusion work that had been identified by the Arts Council. These were:

- community-led work (model 1)
- organisations supported through the former Arts Council and Regional Arts Boards, for whom working with people from low income communities was a mainstay of their work (model 2)
- partnerships brokered by the Arts Council between established, funded organisations with little or no experience of working with people and communities in low income areas, and organisations with a track record of work in this field (model 3)

However, in practice none of the case study projects could be described as 'community-led' – all had been initiated by staff in arts organisations or in the Arts Council or Regional Arts Boards.

Methods

A literature review, *The Arts and Social Exclusion: a review prepared for the Arts Council of England* (Jermyn, 2001), was conducted to inform the production of a research framework to guide data collection and analysis. The resulting framework divided into two areas:

- practice – which identified themes that had previously been identified as influencing a successful outcome
- outcomes – which grouped outcomes that had previously been identified in studies and suggested possible indicators that might be used to measure success

The research methods included interviews with arts staff, participants and stakeholders, observation of projects in action and analysis of organisations' own evaluations. Interviews were conducted with:

- 66 artists and other staff working in or for arts organisations
- 53 participants, including 31 who were interviewed using a specially designed questionnaire at the end of projects

- nine coordinators or leaders of groups participating in projects
- eight other stakeholders such as representatives from participating schools, evaluators and health workers

Key findings

Definitions and language

One of the fundamental issues to arise from the research concerned definitions and language. Some arts practitioners talked about 'social inclusion', some talked about 'social exclusion', and some were unsure what the correct terminology was. While 'social inclusion' was felt to be less offensive and more palatable than 'social exclusion', practitioners did not feel comfortable with this language.

The research documented a broad range of arts practice but raises the question of whether it all counts as 'social inclusion work'. Some projects targeted groups that some might define as 'socially excluded' or at risk of exclusion, such as young offenders, homeless people or recovering drug addicts. Other projects targeted geographic areas or neighbourhoods that were identified as experiencing social exclusion (because they ranked highly in deprivation indices, for example). But arts projects were not necessarily seeking *explicitly* to tackle the four policy indicators of social inclusion that are commonly referred to (health, education, employment and crime). The crux of the matter is that arts projects involving work with excluded groups or in excluded communities can have different purposes – for some, a key purpose may be to use the arts to address certain problems associated with social exclusion, while other work may have no such social objectives and be offered purely as an opportunity to participate in arts activities.

Good practice principles in delivering 'social inclusion work'

For the purposes of this research all the case study projects have been counted as part of the 'social inclusion work' continuum.

For artists delivering projects
Artists used a number of recurrent principles when delivering projects with excluded groups or in areas of exclusion:

- having flexible and adaptable working methods. That flexibility was evident in various ways in arts practice:
  - artists had goals but there was flexibility in the route taken to reach these
  - artists adapted their methods to accommodate individuals' different strengths, ideas and needs
  - artists adapted the pace to suit participants
  - artists had a 'toolkit' of ideas and approaches (if one approach did not work they would try another)
- working collaboratively with participants – all projects had a democratic dimension but an 'anything goes' approach was not evident; indeed some of the activity was strongly led or directed
- pursuing quality – both in the process and outcome
- responding to individuals' needs – this sometimes had implications in terms of needing more than one artist leading activity or costing in the support of someone with specialist skills, such as a youth worker, for example. The importance of being able to give participants one-to-one attention was a recurrent theme

For those planning and coordinating projects
Projects could be successful, in terms of the work taking place in sessions and participant outcomes, even when difficulties were being experienced with the nuts and bolts of running the project. However, certain 'good practice' principles helped projects run smoothly and supported the achievement of positive outcomes:

- building in time to plan and research projects. For example, time was needed to develop appropriate recruitment strategies and lay the foundations for successful partnership working
- setting clear and realistic aims and objectives that are worked through in terms of delivery and understood by all partners, including the artists responsible for leading arts activity. Building in mechanisms for measuring objectives, and, if those aims and objectives are to be used as a tool for monitoring and developing projects, revisiting them while the project is in progress not just when the project has ended
- incorporating appropriate participant recruitment strategies. Many of the projects in the research involved artists working with pre-existing groups on their 'home territory'. Those that did not, tended to incorporate face-to-face contact as part of the recruitment process (for example, artists went to meet potential participants or delivered a taster session before encouraging people

to move to a different environment). The design of projects should acknowledge that the move from a familiar to an unfamiliar territory is a significant step for some groups and that recruitment can be a time-consuming process – it can take a while to build up trust, for word of mouth to spread and for a project to gain momentum

- supporting people's participation by meeting their practical needs eg covering travel costs, providing a crèche, supplying food or food vouchers
- adopting procedures that protect the safety of artists and participants
- building robust partnerships (see below)
- ensuring sustainability, or alternatively exit strategies, are considered early on in the development of a project and then worked through (see below)
- having a clear evaluation strategy. *Sharing Practice* (Moriarty, 2002) provides useful guidance on developing a strategic approach to evaluation. The research found that evaluation was most effective when it was built into projects from the start rather than dealt with in a relatively ad hoc way once projects were under way
- where appropriate, creating a working structure which supports the effective working of freelance artists eg ensuring they are supported in their work, informed about policies and know what is expected of them
- equipping projects with the appropriate staff and resources

Partnerships

There were four model 3 partnerships but several of the other case study projects also involved partnerships and these were considered in the research. Many of the challenges experienced by the model 3 partnerships were generic issues that affected other partnerships.

Partnership can mean many different things. Within the research there were examples of arts partners that worked largely independently of each other, and ones that worked more closely, but where there was a strict demarcation of roles and responsibilities. Partnerships with non-arts partners ranged from those in which agencies did little more than 'host' arts activities to those where there were very active and committed agencies.

Common problems experienced in partnerships included communication difficulties (eg lines of communication were not clear, misunderstandings happened, things were not communicated at all) and a lack of clarity about roles and responsibilities. There were examples of non-arts agencies taking a very passive role and this had a negative impact on the success of projects.

Committed partners tended to have the opposite effect. In addition, partnerships often relied on individual 'enthusiasts' (either artists or staff and volunteers within agencies or communities). Inevitably, when an individual departed mid-project, this often had a negative impact.

Partnership projects highlighted the importance of:

- setting clear aims and objectives that were understood by partners
- delivering projects that fitted naturally with organisations' respective goals
- being realistic about the level of contribution individual partners could make
- discussing how the partnership would work, particularly as organisations can be so different. For example, in the research there were partners who were coming from different places and had different organisational objectives (eg a venue perspective or a community arts perspective), had different ways of working (eg 'organic' or ordered), or were very different in size (eg large organisations with many departments and specialised functions, or small organisations where one or two people did everything)
- creating strong partnerships with non-arts agencies

Sustainability

Discussions about sustainability were relevant both in terms of the continuity of participants' engagement in the arts and developing 'the sector'. However, there were a number of barriers that meant achieving sustainability was difficult. These included:

- funding issues – organisations that wanted to work in a more strategic way and offer pathways for progression were hampered from doing so by difficulties with funding, which tended to be project-orientated. Further, the levels of investment required were sometimes high (because of the high ratio of artists to participants, for example). Funders were felt to be more interested in supporting 'innovation' and things that were 'new' rather than enabling activity to continue
- weak partnerships – practitioners felt that developing partnerships with non-arts agencies might be one way to secure sustainability but the partnerships that formed were sometimes weak and non-arts agencies were not always the committed partners arts organisations had hoped for
- dependence of work on a limited pool of individual artists and small organisations. Some interviewees felt there was a shortage of artists with the

necessary skills to work in this area. During the course of the research some organisations appeared stretched to manage the expansion of work
- arts organisations did not always tackle the sustainability issue seriously enough, early enough. For example, there were examples of organisations that acknowledged from the start that this issue had to be addressed but only took action to achieve this (such as approaching potential partners or applying for funding) at a late stage in the project's development.

The problem of 'what next?' was a difficult issue for many artists and project coordinators who felt they had a moral duty not to 'parachute in' to communities, deliver a project and then run. Organisations that had no plans to offer pathways for progression handled the closure of projects in various ways:

- it was felt important not to raise expectation that activity would continue and to make promises that could not be kept
- projects were ended in a positive way – through a trip to see an exhibition of their work or a certificate presentation, for example
- one organisation had built in a post-project debrief where participants came together to talk about their experience

There were some examples of organisations offering participants some form of continuity, eg developing programmes of work rather than 'one-off' projects; supporting the development of regular groups that stemmed from one-off projects; and the creation of a 'drop-in' facility that could be used by participants. Other approaches to continuity included: building a training or mentoring element into projects in the hope that people within groups would be inspired to lead activities themselves; inviting participants to open access events; keeping participants informed of events run by other organisations that might be of interest. More generally, organisations would signpost people on to other groups or classes but, as interviewees pointed out, this was often an unsatisfactory approach.

Success indicators

Meeting aims and objectives
One possible indicator of success might be to assess projects according to whether they have achieved their objectives. A scan through the 15 research case studies reveals how much variation there was in the nature of objectives set by organisations. Some could be achieved relatively easily, some were challenging and some were unrealistic; some focused on reaching certain

numbers of people, on an end product such as a play or on less tangible outcomes (such as raised self-esteem). Therefore, judging the success of projects according to whether they have met their aims and objectives is problematic because one is not comparing like with like. Further, artists wanted to do more than achieve objectives at all costs or 'on paper' only and there were good reasons why certain objectives were not pursued in practice.

Achieving certain outcomes
The research sought to test potential 'success indicators', which involved exploring the outcomes that have previously been identified as potential outcomes of arts participation. A participant survey was administered by the researcher which allowed certain qualitative outcomes to be quantified but also offered latitude to discuss some areas in more depth than a purely indicator-based approach would allow. One of the difficulties underlying an indicator-based approach is that there is such a diversity of work taking place, with particular groups having particular needs, and a one-size-fits-all approach will inevitably be problematic. Further, while it is possible to quantify certain outcomes (such as increases in confidence), the indicators can be ambiguous and need to be interpreted with care. For example, if someone feels no more confident at the end of the project than at the start that does not mean the project has 'failed'. Indicators in themselves can only tell us so much.

Because of the small sample of projects and participants it is difficult to generalise to a wider population, but participation in the arts had the following effects for some participants:

- raised levels of self-esteem and confidence – as a result of projects, participants said they felt proud of what they had achieved, felt more confident and many felt better about themselves
- a greater feeling of self-determination and sense of control – participants felt they had had freedom to develop their ideas and, although fewer participants felt they had had a say over what happened in sessions, they generally felt a strong sense of ownership of the final product
- pleasure and enjoyment
- more developed arts and creative skills, appreciation of the arts, positive attitudes to the arts and a taste for more

As noted above, projects tended not to have aims that involved 'tackling' the problems associated with social exclusion. However, soft outcomes such as confidence have been identified as indicators of 'distance travelled' towards certain 'hard' outcomes such as employment.

There were also project-specific outcomes which would be best 'measured' by project-specific indicators. For example, a drama project aimed to complement the recovery process for a group of recovering drug addicts, a prison-based project used literature as a tool to develop prisoners' understanding of themselves, and a visual arts project for young homeless people hoped to support their move into more structured learning.

Practitioners' perceptions of success
Artists themselves would sometimes judge the success of projects by referring to the seemingly small, but significant, developments they had witnessed among participants. Examples mentioned in the research included:

- a participant printing out his name without any help
- a person borrowing a book from the library because he had enjoyed reading an excerpt from it during a project
- participants arriving early for sessions and asking for sessions to be longer

The artists would also reflect on whether the group had met its potential, and on the progression of the group and of individuals. The judgements made by others, be they audiences, attenders or other groups, also informed artists' perceptions of whether a project had been a success or not.

What next?

The research has possibly raised more questions than it answers but future discussion might usefully focus on the following:

- how can we more effectively communicate about this work? A good starting point might be for the Arts Council to consider whether it can offer a clearer definition of social exclusion than the one it offers in *Addressing social exclusion: a framework for action* (Arts Council of England, 1999) and outline what it counts as 'social inclusion work' eg does it incorporate work with socially excluded groups or in areas of social exclusion that do not have social objectives? Is it different from access? How does it relate to audience development?

- how can we best disseminate and share good practice in this area of work? Such dissemination needs to reach not only arts organisations but also freelance artists and potential partners
- would a code of practice for artists working with vulnerable and volatile groups be valuable?
- how can the Arts Council and other funders best support organisations seeking to develop programmes of work and offer participants opportunities to continue engaging with the arts?
- from a funder's point of view, what are the best strategies for securing sustainable activity? For example, relatively high levels of investment were made to some projects through the New Audiences Programme which had 'long-term' aspirations but, at that initial stage, could the Arts Council have done more to increase the chances of realising those aims?
- how can we best build a strong 'sector' eg in terms of supporting artists' training and development, the development of emerging organisations and the development of existing organisations? The development of awareness and understanding of arts work among workers in potential partner agencies (such as youth workers, youth offending teams etc) is also relevant
- how can we best support the development of robust partnerships with non-arts agencies?
- is an indicator-based approach a viable way of measuring the success of projects in a sector where practice is so diverse and the purposes of projects so wide? If such a measure is to be used, guidance is needed on which indicators would be both practical and meaningful for the arts organisations involved

In addition, potential avenues for future research might include the following:

- impact – rigorous research that specifically looks at the impact of projects that explicitly aim to affect health, crime, education, employment and community regeneration
- exploring community-led projects to complement this research. Here, social capital theories might usefully be used to explore longer-term community orientated projects
- longitudinal research that explores participation in the arts and its longer-term impact

1 Introduction

1.1 Context

The Social Exclusion Unit (SEU) was established in December 1997 with a remit to improve Government action to reduce social exclusion by producing 'joined up solutions to joined up problems'. For the SEU social exclusion is 'a shorthand term for what can happen when people or areas suffer from a combination of linked problems such as unemployment, poor skills, low incomes, poor housing, high crime environments, bad health and family breakdown' (Cabinet Office, 1998).

Bringing Britain Together: a national strategy for neighbourhood renewal (Cabinet Office, 1998) described the concentration in poor neighbourhoods of a range of interlocking problems such as high levels of unemployment, crime, ill-health and poor education. Following its publication, 18 Policy Action Teams (PATs) were established to take forward work in key policy areas. PAT 10, chaired by the Department for Culture, Media and Sport (DCMS), explored good practice in using arts, sport and leisure to engage people in poor neighbourhoods, and how to maximise the impact on poor neighbourhoods of Government spending and polices on arts, sport and leisure.

PAT 10's report to the SEU (DCMS, 1999) concluded that arts, sport and cultural and recreational activity can contribute to neighbourhood renewal and make a real difference to health, crime, employment and education in deprived communities. The team suggested this was because such activities:

- appeal directly to individuals' interests and develop their potential and self-confidence
- relate to community identity and encourage collective effort
- help build positive links with the wider community
- are associated with rapidly growing industries

In response to PAT 10, the Arts Council produced *Addressing social exclusion: a framework for action* (1999) which identified five key ways in which it would take forward its work in social inclusion: profile raising; the work of regularly funded organisations[1]; evaluation; multi-agency working; and targeting resources (ACE,

---

[1] Regularly funded organisations are organisations that receive funding from the Arts Council on an ongoing basis from grant-in-aid. The Arts Council has a funding agreement with these organisations and regularly reviews them to ensure the funds invested in them are meeting the terms of their funding agreement.

1999). The Arts Council has gone on to use some programmes to support its social inclusion objectives. For example, £720,000 was allocated to projects through the Social Inclusion strand of the New Audiences Programme, one of five strands of work supported by the final phase of the programme, and £40 million was used to work with schools in some of the most economically and socially challenged areas in England through the first phase of Creative Partnerships. The social inclusion team at the Arts Council's national office has focused activity in two key areas: criminal justice and health.

The Public Sector Agreement (PSA) targets that DCMS has agreed with the Treasury for 2003-6 are also of relevance. PSA target 2 is 'increase significantly take-up of cultural and sporting opportunities by new users aged 20 and above from priority groups' and Arts Council England, as a non-departmental body sponsored by DCMS, has in turn agreed targets that will contribute to this goal. The Arts Council has identified three 'priority groups': socially excluded groups, disabled people and Black and minority ethnic people. Progress towards achieving the targets is being measured through a survey of attendance and participation.

1.2 Research background

One of the very specific issues raised in the PAT 10 report, and in subsequent reviews of the literature (eg Coalter, 2001), was the lack of evaluation illustrating the impact of the arts. Subsequently, the Arts Council commissioned several research projects and evaluations in the area of arts and social exclusion. Much of this work, including this research study, was supported through the New Audiences Programme.

In January 2001 the former Arts Council of England and Regional Arts Boards[2] commissioned research to test three models of social inclusion work occurring in the arts:
- model 1 was community-led work, where the initiative for the arts project came from a local community or group
- model 2 covered experienced arts organisations or companies supported through the former Arts Council and Regional Arts Boards, for whom working with people from low income communities was a mainstay of their work
- model 3 were partnerships brokered by the Arts Council between established, funded organisations with little or no experience of working with people and

---

[2] On 1 April 2002 the Arts Council of England and the 10 Regional Arts Boards joined together to form a single development organisation for the arts – Arts Council England.

communities in low income areas, and organisations with a track record of work in this field

The research comprised two discrete, but related, strands of work:

- self-evaluation: working with organisations to help them evaluate their own practice and developing an evaluation guide which could be used by arts organisations undertaking work in the area of social exclusion
- external evaluation: an overarching research project exploring arts practice and outcomes

The Arts Council commissioned Gerri Moriarty, a community artist and arts consultant, to lead the self-evaluation strand of work and the resulting report, *Sharing practice: a guide to self-evaluation for artists, arts organisations and funders working in the context of social exclusion*, was published in 2002.[3] Helen Jermyn, an independent researcher, was commissioned to conduct the external evaluation and this report presents key findings of that work.

1.3   Project aims

The overall objectives of the research were to:

- gather evidence that could be used to inform policy and advocacy initiatives
- develop and test appropriate methodologies for evaluating arts initiatives with aims relating to social inclusion
- evaluate three different models of initiating and delivering projects
- identify the characteristics of successful initiatives
- identify approaches that do not work and the reasons for this
- develop measures of success that could be used to evaluate a broad range of initiatives

1.4   Selection of participating organisations and projects

Initially, the then Regional Arts Boards nominated organisations (and in some cases specific projects) which they felt exemplified good practice in social inclusion work; 18 organisations and projects were nominated and they each

---

[3] The report was published on the New Audiences website:
http://www.newaudiences.org.uk/static/news_story_20030701_4.html

received a sum of £2,000 from the New Audiences Programme to cover the costs of participating in the work.[4]

In addition, the research sample included four national-led 'model 3' projects. These were partnership projects brokered by the Arts Council national office which were awarded a total of £140,000 from the Social Inclusion strand of the New Audiences Programme. The Social Inclusion strand also funded 14 regional 'Enabling Inclusion' projects, which together received a total of £331,244; half of these regional projects were added to the external evaluation in January 2002.

It was hoped that all the nominated and model 3 organisations would participate in both the self-evaluation and external evaluation strands of the research programme. All participated in the self-evaluation strand and contributed to *Sharing Practice* (Moriarty, 2002) but five did not go on to participate in the external evaluation, for a variety of reasons. The most common reason was that organisations experienced some change in circumstances during the course of the project, such as the departure of a key worker or an expansion in work, which made their participation in the research difficult.

Twenty-eight arts organisations[5] participated in the research:

- 11 organisations had either been nominated by Regional Arts Boards directly or were partners in projects where one organisation had been nominated:
  - Bournemouth Theatre in Education*[6]
  - City Arts and Angel Row Gallery (although it was Nottingham Partnership Council, a regeneration organisation, that supported this project which was nominated by the arts board)*
  - Community Music East
  - Darts
  - Fusion*
  - Horn Reflections*
  - Jubilee Arts
  - Same Sky

---

[4] Three of the 18 organisations originally nominated by Regional Arts Boards went on to be involved in the model 3 partnerships or one of the other projects funded through the Social Inclusion strand of New Audiences ie Cardboard Citizens, Seachange and Mantle Arts.

[5] This includes one writer in residence post, classified here as "arts organisation".

[6] * Indicates that a project case study is available. Appendix 1 includes the case studies for Bournemouth Theatre in Education, HMP Channings Wood, Artsworks-mk and Milton Keynes Gallery, and Eastern Touring Agency and Mercury Theatre. All the case studies are available [online} from: http://www.newaudiences.org.uk.

- o Soft Touch*
- o Writer in residence at HMP Channings Wood*
- eight were involved in four model 3 projects:
  - o Artworks-mk and Milton Keynes Gallery*[7]
  - o Birmingham Opera and Optima
  - o Cardboard Citizens and Royal Shakespeare Company (RSC)*
  - o Eastern Touring Agency (ETA) (now known as Momentum Arts) and Mercury Theatre*
- and 10 were involved in seven regional projects funded through the New Audience Programme[8]:
  - o Arts About Manchester and Community Arts North West*
  - o Dot to Dot*
  - o Magic Carpet*
  - o Mantle Arts and Charnwood Arts*
  - o Middlesbrough Local Arts Development Agency (LADA) and Cleveland Craft Centre*
  - o Seachange
  - o Unit for the Arts and Offenders*

The methods used to select organisations and projects for inclusion in this research were very flexible; there was a desire to include a wide range of arts practice and definitions as to what counts as 'social inclusion work' were left open. The projects were initiated in different ways, had different aims and objectives and involved different partnerships. The artists delivering projects had different ways of working and a wide range of arts and crafts were represented including digital arts, textiles, painting, mural making, photography, writing, music-making and drama. Participating groups ranged from older people living in sheltered accommodation to families with children aged under 5. Projects took place in settings ranging from prisons to theatres, from community centres to hostels for the homeless. A rich body of data about practice has emerged due to the diversity of organisations and projects in the sample. However, it proved difficult to explore outcomes in the depth originally planned, partly *because* of the diversity of work represented. For example, the sample included a number of drop-in projects where there were high levels of transience and attendance was erratic – to assess the impact of this project on individuals a very different research approach would be needed.

---

[8] Eighteen projects were funded through enabling inclusion, one of the strands of the New Audiences Programme.

More generally, variable attendance and attrition rates affected the size of the participant statistical base and research tools needed a certain amount of adaptation to suit projects, participants and the interview situation. To guarantee a large sample, the Arts Council would have needed either to be more prescriptive about what types of practice or projects to include, or begin with a far larger sample of projects.

1.5   Structure of report

The main report presents research findings and has 10 chapters. Chapters 2 and 3 provide a context for the research: chapter 2 explores research methodology and chapter 3 considers people's understandings of terms such as social exclusion. Chapter 4 examines the range of arts practice represented in the research and chapter 5 explores the outcomes generated by projects. Chapters 6 to 8 explore in more depth issues including partnership, sustainability, evaluation and good practice. Finally, chapter 9 offers some concluding thoughts.

Fifteen individual project case studies were researched, representing a range of different artforms, types of participants and ways of working (see Table 1 for summary). The researcher has agreed the case studies with the relevant lead organisations who have, in the spirit of *Sharing Practice* (Moriarty, 2002), shown a willingness to share with others the lessons they have learned. Four of the case studies are included in Appendix 1; all 15 are available from Arts Council England's website.

Table 1: Summary of 15 case studies

Case study	Lead organisation(s)	Artform	Project summary	Targeted participants
1	Writer in residence at HMP Channings Wood	Literature	*Connections* A group of prisoners attended a 10-week literature course facilitated by staff. The ethos behind the project was that, in understanding the characters in the texts, participants would understand themselves better.	Male prisoners
2	Bournemouth Theatre in Education	Drama	*Vita Nova* Vita Nova is a theatre group of recovering drug addicts. The case study examines the role the project has played in members' ongoing recovery and focuses on their adaptation of Shakespeare's *A Midsummer Night's Dream*, a collaboration involving Vita Nova and Dorset Police.	People in recovery from addiction to drugs
3	Fusion	Crafts and visual arts	*Fast Forward* A two-year arts programme was developed in partnership with homeless agencies and social care providers. Young homeless people participated in a programme of arts outreach, workshops and accredited education.	Homeless people
4	Horn Reflections	Drama	*The Treatment* A group of young people devised, rehearsed and performed a play that explored health issues. The project aimed to attract young people with an interest in the arts of the people of Africa.	Young people

5	Eastern Touring Agency (ETA) and Mercury Theatre (model 3)	Drama	*ETA and Mercury Theatre model 3 project* The Arts Council research focused on the 2001 summer residency for young offenders. The group worked with a director and two professional actors to devise, rehearse and perform a play, *Landed*.	Young offenders
6	Artworks-mk and Milton Keynes Gallery (model 3)	Photography and visual arts	*Fashion and ID* Younger and older residents living on a Milton Keynes housing estate participated in photography and mixed media workshops led by two artists. The participants' work was exhibited at the Gallery and in the window of an Artworks-MK workshop located on the estate.	Young and older people living on housing estate in Milton Keynes
7	Cardboard Citizens and the RSC (model 3)	Drama	*Pericles* Cardboard Citizens collaborated with the RSC to deliver outreach workshops for refugee and homeless groups and to use those experiences to inform a production of *Pericles*. The project involved working with and producing work by homeless and ex-homeless people.	Refugees, homeless and ex-homeless people
8	Charnwood Arts and Mantle Arts	Visual arts	*eState of the Art* Young people from five estates participated in a programme of visual arts and music activities. A website provided a way of sharing work and experiences across the estates.	Young people living on housing estates in Coalville and Loughborough
9	Dot to Dot	Various including music, visual arts and	*Telling Tales* A project coordinator was appointed to support arts development in Ventnor, Isle of	Families living in Ventnor and local artists

		crafts. Training.	Wight. Families participated in a varied programme of arts events and activities, including carnival costume making, samba, music, book making and batik. Training was also offered to local artists; this included a supervised SureStart training programme in working with children aged under 5.	
10	Middlesbrough LADA and Cleveland Craft Centre	Jewellery and textiles	*Thorntree Glitter* Family groups designed and made their own jewellery, participated in crafts workshops and displayed their work in a professionally curated exhibition at Cleveland Craft Centre. The project included a residency led by jeweller, Laura Potter. As part of the residency Potter was commissioned to produce a piece of jewellery for the Centre's permanent jewellery collection.	Families living in Thorntree
11	Arts About Manchester and North West Community Arts	Various artforms	*Open House* Six participatory arts groups were offered opportunities to visit different art galleries, theatres and museums across Greater Manchester. A CD-ROM telling the story of *Open House* and documenting the groups' visits was produced.	Local community groups
12	City Arts and The Angel Row Gallery (project supported through Nottingham Partnership Council)	Crafts, visual arts and writing	*Residence* Two artists, a jeweller/metal worker and a writer, worked with groups in the NG7 area of Nottingham to produce original writing and objects around the theme of 'home'. Participants customised plain wooden boxes	Users of a drop-in community centre and a mental health group

			to create unique pieces that combined metalwork with text. A selection of participants' work was exhibited at Angel Row Gallery and at the Arts Exchange Gallery.	
13	Unit for the Arts and Offenders	Continuing professional development	*Training for artists* The Unit for the Arts and Offenders designed and piloted two courses: a course for people interested in working with vulnerable and volatile groups; and a course providing specialist training for those wishing to work in a criminal justice context.	Professional artists in South East
14	Soft Touch	Digital arts	*Youthweb* Verve, a group of young people with physical, sensory and learning disabilities, worked with Soft Touch to create the content for a website. The site gave young people the opportunity to voice their opinions and feelings about issues which affected their lives.	Organised group for people with disabilities
15	Magic Carpet	Visual arts and crafts, drama, writing and mixed media	*Developing partnerships between arts organisations and social providers* Three community groups in Exeter participated in a workshop programme including visual arts and crafts, drama, writing and words, and mixed media. The project tested different models of working by targeting three different types of group.	Users of a community drop-in centre, a drugs information service and a mental health group

2 Methodology

This chapter describes how a literature review was used to create a research framework which guided data collection and analysis. It also considers some of the methodological challenges involved in this area of work and the research approach.

2.1 Use of a literature review to create a research framework

As outlined in chapter 1, the research aimed to test different models of social inclusion work occurring in the arts and the external evaluation strand involved looking at arts practice and outcomes. The organisations and projects participating in the research were so diverse it was important to create an overarching framework that could be used to guide data collection and analysis. The research, therefore, began with a literature review (Jermyn, 2001) which was used to inform the development of such a framework.

The review was commissioned with the specific purpose of exploring the policy context and informing the design of the research. It was not intended to be an exhaustive review of all the literature in this field. Areas covered included:

- factors that contribute to a successful outcome
- the claimed impacts of the arts
- the methodologies that have been used to evaluate arts projects and the methodological challenges raised through such work

The resulting research framework had two main areas of interest, both of which are considered in more depth below:

- documenting and exploring the range of arts practice
- assessing project outcomes

Since the publication of the review, a number of other relevant pieces of research and reviews have been published such as *Measuring the economic and social impact of the arts* (Reeves, 2002), *Count me in – the dimensions of social inclusion through culture and sport* (Leeds Metropolitan University, 2002), *A Review of evaluation in community-based art for health activity in the UK* (Angus, 2002) and *Doing the arts justice: a literature review of arts practice in the criminal justice system* compiled by the Centre for Applied Theatre Research (Miles and McLewin, 2004).

2.2 Good practice

The literature that has identified good practice principles underpinning social inclusion work in the arts has often been accompanied by caveats that there is no single winning formula. Jermyn (2001) noted the 'lack of rigorous analysis of what works' but identified a number of recurrent principles which commentators had identified as influencing a successful outcome (Table 2):

- **Connecting with local needs**: For example, the Health Development Agency's (HDA, 2000) review of arts and health projects found that good practice clearly identified and articulated local need (though seldom through formal means)
- **Control, equitable partnerships and flexible working methods**: Carpenter (1999), in her evaluation of a number of projects involving the arts and socially excluded communities, concluded that the more democratic the relationship between the artist and audience or participant, the more successful the project appeared to be in reaching and engaging significant numbers of people.[9] The implications for practitioners arising from Carpenter's work include a willingness on the part of artists and other staff to share control with participants, and the use of flexible and adaptable working methods
- **Project planning and resources**: The HDA (2000) found all good practice case studies had enough time for planning, for building successful participatory methodologies and creating robust models for partnership working. Carpenter (1999), Matarasso (1997) and others have also highlighted the importance of project planning and inputting enough resources
- **Quality, excellence or pride in achievement**: These were recurrent themes; indeed the HDA review noted that an 'anything goes' attitude could be detrimental to a project's success

There are likely to be other factors that influence a successful outcome that are less easily identified and articulated. As someone commenting on a draft of the review said, factors such as creative passion, dynamic interrelationships, tough love, imaginative and unplanned experimentation and innovative problem-solving, may not appear on good practice lists but they are relevant nevertheless.

---

[9] Carpenter drew analysis criteria from theories about the democratic process.

Table 2: Good practice principles

PAT 10 (DCMS, 1999)	Williams (1997)	Matarasso (1997)
• defining common objectives in relation to actual needs	• clearly stated objectives	• clear objectives
• promoting equitable partnerships • supporting local commitment • embedding local control	• group ownership, trust and cooperation • meaningful levels of participation • artists as collaborators	• equitable partnerships
• pursuing quality across the spectrum	• pride in artistic achievement	• excellence
• securing sustainability • connecting with the mainstream of art and sport activities • working flexibly with change • valuing diversity	• degree of investment by other stakeholders in the long-term outcomes • degree of goodwill developed in other allied local or regional organisations and networks • capacity to develop community leadership	• shared ethical principles • proportional expectations • good planning • joint evaluation

Source: DCMS, 1999; Williams, 1997; Matarasso, 1997. Cited in Jermyn, 2001.

There are also factors that may have a negative influence on outcomes. Moriarty (1998) noted the over-dependence on a limited number of individuals who have experience of working with marginalised groups. The HDA (2000) noted that the most successful arts-based interventions were often based on the intuition of an individual who acted as an impetus for the project's conception, development and deployment. The dependence on a limited number of artists and organisations will have implications on the sustainability of work in this field. Further barriers identified by PAT 10 (DCMS, 1999) included: projects being tailored to programme or policy criteria rather than community needs, and short-term perspectives; and poor links between arts and sports bodies and major players such as schools.

The 'good practice' principles identified through the review were used as a framework for data collection and analysis (Table 3). The research sought to explore these principles rather than take them as proven criteria. For example, 'responding to needs' and 'flexibility' have been identified as principles influencing a successful outcome but what do these mean in practice?

Table 3: Research framework - good practice themes

Recurrent good practice principles	The sorts of questions investigated
1 Sufficient time, planning, resources, equitable partnerships	What steps do projects take in planning projects? What factors are considered in working with participants? What factors (in terms of planning) contribute to a 'successful' project or enhance outcomes? What external and internal factors result in project plans changing or reduce the impact of outcomes? What models of partnership working are effective or not effective?
2 Embedded local control, connecting to community needs	How, if at all, do organisations identify the needs of participants? How, if at all, do projects develop in response to needs?
3 Clear objectives, evaluation	How, if at all, are aims and objectives set? What, if any, social objectives are identified and are participants made aware of desired outcomes? How do projects intend to achieve social objectives? How, if at all, are objectives evaluated? How do aims and objectives change, if at all, over time?
4 Flexibility	How is flexibility an issue in participant-artist relationship and in the arts process?

5 Issues around ownership, control of agenda, artist as collaborator	How are participants involved in the process (from project concept through to implementation and evaluation)? What are the dynamics between artist, participants and partners in controlling the agenda and directing the project? How do participants make views known or influence direction of project (any formal mechanisms)? What is the nature of participation (ie type of activity, intensity, challenge/risk taking, level of directed activity, relevance)?
6 Values and principles	What principles, if any, underpin work that aims to be socially inclusive? How do principles translate into practice?
7 Importance of quality, pride in achievement	Do participants and artists regard 'excellence' or 'quality' as important? What do they understand by these terms? Is there a relationship between benefits derived from arts participation and pride in achievement?
8 Sustainability and legacy	Do projects consider the longer term legacy of projects? Are steps taken to provide lasting benefits to participants? What exit strategies exist (any form of progression or continuing support for participants)? What are the sustainability issues in terms of organisational resources?

2.3   Project outcomes

Jermyn (2001) also looked at some of the literature concerned with the social impact of the arts and research concerned with the arts and social inclusion. Although much of the existing social impact research was not concerned specifically with social exclusion, it was included in the review because the methodologies adopted and outcomes identified were relevant to the Arts Council study.[10]

Policy makers, arts practitioners and researchers have suggested that participation in arts activity can result in a broad range of positive effects; these range from increased self-confidence to increased educational attainment, from social cohesion to reduced offending behaviour (Table 4 and Appendix 2).

Some of the claimed benefits derived from the arts, such as self-esteem, are primarily personal or individual benefits, while others, such as developing community identity, occur at a community level. It has been suggested that those participating in arts programmes may accrue some benefits (such as self-esteem or creative skills) directly as a result of their participation (ie arts + participation = outcome). However, there are also processes that are less direct and more complex and are dependent on achieving intermediary outcomes. For example, people may learn new skills and feel more confident as the result of participating in community arts activity, and this, in turn, may increase their employability.

---

[10] Concerns have been expressed that social impact research had tended to become confused with research into the role of the arts in addressing social exclusion eg *Measuring the Impact of Culture*, seminar, June 2000, Arts Research Digest Ltd.

Table 4: Selection of claimed impacts of the arts

Claimed impacts of the arts
Individual
• develop self-confidence and self-esteem
• increase creativity and thinking skills
• improve skills in planning and organising activities
• improve communication of ideas and information
• raise or enhance educational attainment
• increase appreciation of arts
• enhance mental and physical health and well-being
• increase the employability of individuals
• reduce offending behaviour
• alleviate the impact of poverty
Group/community
• create social capital
• decrease social isolation
• improve understanding of different cultures
• strengthen communities
• enhance social cohesion
• develop community identity
• promote interest in the local environment
• activate social change
• raise public awareness of an issue
• contribute to urban regeneration

Source: Landry et al, 1996; Williams, 1996 & 1997; Matarasso, 1997; DCMS, 1999; Blake Stevenson Ltd, 2000; Harland et al, 2000.

Many of the benefits are interlinked, overlapping or even inter-dependent. For example, social capital is a term that is very closely related to social cohesion and well being. Definitions of social capital often refer to the existence of, and participation in, organised networks or groups and less tangible concepts such as social trust, civic cooperation, reciprocity, local democracy and group solidarity. The HDA (2000) has noted the development of social capital theories that place emphasis on social inclusion and connectedness as key determinants of health and well being.

The framework categorised the outcomes identified through the review into four main categories: personal; collective; community; and 'hard' outcomes (Table 5). It corresponded fairly closely with the framework that was developed independently by Leeds Metropolitan University around the same time for a study it was conducting on behalf of DCMS (Leeds Metropolitan University, 2002). Not all outcomes were relevant to all projects participating in the research.

Table 5: Research framework – categorisation of project outcomes

Outcomes	Indicators
'Hard' outcomes	Such as improved health, higher levels of educational attainment, crime reduction
Personal impacts/human capital impacts that individual participants derived from arts experience	• Increased self-confidence • Feel better about themselves, sense of satisfaction, enhanced self-esteem • Feeling of self-determination and sense of control • Pleasure and enjoyment • Arts inclusion (contact where none or little previously, enhanced creative skills, increased arts knowledge, changed attitudes if previously negative) • Acquisition of other skills (eg communication, completing tasks and seeing things through to end, computer and technology, attendance and reliability, planning and problem solving) • Future outlook (broadened horizons, employment prospects, education prospects)
Collective/group impacts impacts derived from social relations with other individuals or groups as part of arts experience	• More social contact (new acquaintances, friends etc) • Increased understanding and tolerance of other people (different generations, cultures, areas) • Group identity and pride (belonging to team, pride, expression of group identity) • Skills (teamwork, social)
Civic/community impacts impacts that go beyond individual or group	• Community belonging and involvement • Community identity and pride • Active community – people co-operating and working together to generate social change • Local democracy – involvement in decision making and control by residents

2.4 Methodological challenges

The review informing this study highlighted a number of challenges inherent in researching the impacts of the arts, many of which were present in other areas of social research enquiry:

- **Clarity of outcomes**: Matarasso (1996) suggested that the first difficulty faced by many arts projects with social objectives is a lack of clarity about which outcomes are intended. It is worth noting that many arts projects do not regard 'hard' social impacts as a primary intended outcome of their work. Also, some organisations prefer to distance themselves from predefining what the social impact of their work will be
- **Conceptual confusion**: terms such as confidence, social capital and community are commonly referred to but they are often used inconsistently and such concepts are sometimes operationalised in different ways
- **Appropriate ways of measuring outcomes**: specific, clear and measurable outcomes may not in themselves reflect the complexity of social impacts. There are also difficulties associated with formally and objectively measuring certain types of personal impacts such as changes in levels of confidence or motivation.[11] Further, measuring progress towards 'hard' outcomes such as employment and establishing the transferability of impacts can be a challenging methodological task
- **Lack of an established methodology**: the HDA (2000) review noted 'there are to date no established principles and protocols for evaluating outcomes, assessing the processes by which outcomes are achieved, and disseminating recommendations for good practice to field workers'. This is equally true of the arts sector more generally
- **Measuring progress**: establishing a baseline or starting point may be difficult (and impossible if outcomes are not predicted), as can quantification of progress. There are no absolute measures; individuals progress from different baselines at different rates. Further, different organisations delivering projects with similar aims will perceive and measure success differently, making comparative analysis problematic
- **Not all outcomes are immediate**: some outcomes take time to develop and will not register in evaluations that focus on the short term

---

[11] It is difficult to get non-self-report measures of personal and subjective constructs like self-esteem. Measurement systems that have been developed in education, health and other areas of social research, some of which were explored in the research design phase of the Arts Council study, may not be appropriate for use in arts projects.

- **Difficulties establishing cause and effect**: to what extent can an impact be attributed to participation in an arts programme or are there other factors at play? There are further issues about whether such outcomes might also have been produced through participation in other activities (arts activities may have an impact for some people, whereas sports activities may be better for others) or might have occurred anyway
- **Satisfying scientific methods of research**: this is particularly relevant to measuring the success of health outcomes or the use of randomised control trials
- **Sensitivity of evaluation**: evaluation must be sensitively conducted and appropriate for use with the groups concerned.[12] For example, certain methods may undermine the self-determination projects seek to encourage, or be inappropriate for projects that have a democratic or participatory ethos. There are also ethical issues about whether it is right to seek to produce change in another person without their informed consent, and safeguarding individuals' interests (Matarasso, 1996)[13]
- **Lack of skills and resources to carry out evaluations**: arts organisations and artists may not feel they have the necessary skills, time or resources to conduct formal evaluation or may perceive evaluation as being secondary or additional to their main purpose – delivering arts activity

In the Arts Council study, it had been hoped that a before-and-after style research design could be adopted; change could then be measured against baseline data. However, this proved difficult to carry out because of participants' erratic attendance, attrition rates and the 'drop-in' nature of some projects. These problems were further compounded by limitations on research time and desire to create a good rapport with participants (see also chapter 5).

Some organisations found it difficult to find time to participate in the research because of other demands (several experienced an increased volume of work during the research period). Future research projects of this type should probably place more emphasis on gauging organisations' capacity to participate in research.

---

[12] Inappropriate evaluation could undermine the aims of a project. Shaw (1999) outlines the following scenario: asking project participants whether they feel more confident as a result of taking part may suggest that the person was considered to be lacking confidence in the first place.

[13] However, it might be argued that 'informed consent' in the context of agreeing intended outcomes places pressure on participants to 'achieve' and may have negative consequences if participants 'fail'.

There was a significant amount of slippage in the research timetable and the reasons for that slippage tell us something about the pressures facing organisations and practitioners working in this area. For example, at various points organisations gave strong indications a project would soon be happening but either it did not happen when planned or at all. The problems experienced were wide-ranging and included:

- difficulty appointing suitable artists or finding dates when particular artists were available
- changes in staffing within organisations (either the arts organisations or in partner organisations)
- difficulty securing funding for projects
- technical hitches and setbacks such as problems with venue leases
- organisations simply changing their mind about which project they wanted to have included in the research

2.5   Research methods

A variety of research methods were used. They included:

- desk-based analysis of relevant documents and materials about the organisations, the projects, participant groups and partner agencies
- an initial meeting with each project to document the background to the organisation and the project
- attendance at key stages of projects' development (eg performances, exhibitions, evaluation or feedback meetings etc)
- interviews with artists, project staff and key stakeholders
- interviews with project participants
- observation of workshops, rehearsals etc
- use of data collected by organisations as part of their own evaluation

Interviews with artists

A total of 74 different artists, project staff and key stakeholders were interviewed. These interviews were recorded and transcribed except where conditions (such as levels of background noise) made this problematic, in which case notes were taken.

Interview schedules were developed for all interviews (see Appendix 3). Artists and project coordinators tended to be interviewed both at the start and at the end of projects; the early interviews focused more heavily on project initiation and planning, while later interviews focused on issues such as outcomes, evaluation, sustainability and lessons learned.

Interviews with participants

Fifty-three individuals participating in projects and nine coordinators of participating groups were interviewed. Most people were interviewed individually although some were interviewed in small groups of two to four people.

Where possible, the researcher sought to conduct individual interviews with participants early on and at the end of projects. The first interview established certain baselines (such as people's previous involvement in the arts) and the second explored what participants felt they had gained from their experience, if anything. A third questionnaire was designed for use in cases where participants had not completed a baseline survey.

In practice, formally interviewing people at the end of projects using the third questionnaire proved to be the most pragmatic approach – 31 participants were interviewed in this way (see Appendix 4). These interviewees were drawn from seven different projects:

- Bournemouth Theatre in Education
- City Arts and Angel Row Gallery
- *Connections*
- ETA and Mercury Theatre
- Fusion
- Horn Reflections
- Soft Touch

Just less than two-thirds of this sample (19 participants) were drawn from three projects (a literature-based project and two drama projects). In the case of five projects, more than half of the participants completing the project were interviewed and the small numbers reflect the fact that projects were working with small numbers of people.

An additional 22 participants and nine coordinators of participating groups were interviewed using specifically designed interview schedules. These interviewees were drawn from projects delivered by:

- Arts About Manchester and Community Arts North West
- Cardboard Citizens and the RSC
- Dot to Dot
- Magic Carpet
- Middlesbrough Arts Council and Cleveland Craft Centre
- Soft Touch

3   Definitions and language

This chapter explores the concept of social exclusion and how it is being used in the arts sector. It also looks at arts practitioners' perceptions of how the arts relate to social exclusion and how they put the concept into practice.

3.1   Definitions of social exclusion

Social exclusion, according to the SEU definition, is complex and multi-dimensional in nature and can occur when various linked problems are experienced in combination.[14] Further, the definition supports a view that social exclusion can be experienced at a range of different levels; it can affect individuals, groups, or geographic areas. The concept is related to, but not the same as, poverty; the Community Development Foundation (CDF, 2001) explains this is because '… it draws attention to people's experiences of being prevented from being full members of society. Social exclusion is more than a material condition'.

The term social exclusion is commonly used in the arts sector but not with consistency. The Arts Council, in *Social exclusion: a framework for action,* agreed on a definition that 'takes low-income areas as its starting point and focuses particularly on poverty in combination with other factors such as low educational attainment, poor health, crime and unemployment' (ACE, 1999). It is perhaps telling that the document noted that 'expanding access has always been an important part of the work of the funding system… Advocating the role the arts can play in addressing social exclusion is however a new departure...' as some organisations and individuals have used access and inclusion synonymously.

Interestingly, a paper commissioned by the Arts Council in 2002, which looked at current thinking on the arts and social inclusion or exclusion within Arts Council England, noted that most of its regional offices were using the term 'social inclusion' (rather than social exclusion) and that officers' first references were to disability and cultural diversity, followed by health and criminal justice; poverty as an underlying concept was rarely mentioned (Shaw, 2003).[15] Meanwhile, the

---

[14] The SEU definition of social exclusion is 'A shorthand term for what can happen when people or areas suffer from a combination of linked problems such as unemployment, poor skills, low incomes, poor housing, high crime environments, bad health and family breakdown' (Cabinet Office, 2000).

[15] The paper (Shaw, 2003) noted that one reason for this may be that officers were working very closely with colleagues who had responsibility for disability and cultural diversity so were more

social inclusion team at Arts Council England, national office, has tended to focus activity in two key areas: health and criminal justice.

Research in the museums sector suggests that the 'fuzziness of the concept social inclusion' was reflected in a 'lack of clarity in some museums and in some local authorities about what counted as social inclusion work' (Group for Large Local Authority Museums, 2000). It follows that any confusion about what social exclusion actually is will impact on organisations' abilities to demonstrate that they are indeed combating or addressing it.

3.2   Social inclusion or social exclusion

While some of the arts practitioners interviewed in the research talked about social inclusion, others talked about social exclusion, and some were unsure what the 'correct' terminology was. The terms social inclusion or social exclusion were used by all the organisations participating in the research but only in the context of funding applications or policy making.

People did not feel comfortable with the language. Social exclusion in particular, was felt to be 'labelling' and stigmatising; as one artist explained, 'people placed in these categories don't feel that they are socially excluded, it's a term you wouldn't use to their faces'. Social inclusion was generally felt to be less offensive and more palatable, although some found the 'social' categorisation difficult in the same way as they felt uncomfortable with the 'cultural' categorisation in 'cultural inclusion'; the objective to 'include' people raised the question – inclusion in whose culture and whose society?

> We use the term social exclusion in grant applications, in letters to the Council and so on. Ex-offenders and other groups we work with are on the outside of society but there's no point in addressing them as socially excluded. We work with people who don't have opportunities, that's the difference between us and a youth theatre.
> Artist

> Is it social exclusion or social inclusion? There are times when we use it [social exclusion] but I don't like it. I don't feel comfortable with the term and its meaning is not clear. We try to avoid using the language with our

conscious of the contribution that they were making to these two fields. Another reason is that in some cases the officer with responsibility for social inclusion shared some responsibility for disability or cultural diversity.

clients, 'I'm working with you because you are socially excluded'. I don't know if people who are categorised as socially excluded feel like they are excluded.
Project coordinator

… people don't want to be labelled. They don't consider themselves to be in need of social inclusion. That's not how they view themselves at all. It's not appropriate to use that kind of language because people would think you were being patronising. So it's purely offered on the basis that it's an opportunity to be involved in a really great project – make pieces of jewellery, have a trip to the V&A, have some work exhibited at the Crafts Centre.
Project partner

[Feels uncomfortable with the language] because the minute you say the word social inclusion then you are telling people that you deem them to be excluded which we don't, we just see them as different people within the community that we want to work with, but we have decided that the relatively well educated, white, middle class folk find it easier to access the arts than other people, and therefore our work has always been targeted at those people who haven't had those opportunities.
Artist

While practitioners did not necessarily like the language, many felt it was just another label for work that community artists had been doing for 15 or 20 years. Some noted the increased interest in this area of work had been beneficial because it provided a forum for debate and had opened up financial resources.

In some ways those phrases are entering the national vocabulary if you like. I think in some ways that's been a bit of a gift for us, in that that's always what we've been about, you know we might talk about the disadvantaged or lacking opportunities, we've always been working with what we find is now social exclusion. But I don't think we have a problem with it. I would have a problem with it if I was talking to kids we were working with.
Artist

I'm only using it because it's trendy language, that's always been the drive – it's about targeting people who don't usually have access to the arts, and that's always been the agenda. But I have problems with it and we don't

26

actually like using the term social inclusion but it comes in dead handy
sometimes.
Project coordinator

3.3   Who is socially excluded?

As noted earlier, social exclusion is a complex concept that encompasses linked
problems and may affect people or areas. Allin (2000) has suggested that there
appears to be some confusion as to whether it is people or areas that suffer
exclusion, while Glass (2000) has posed the question 'do we want to measure
social exclusion or the effects of trying to combat social exclusion?' (eg more or
less social exclusion or more or less teenage pregnancy?). Quite clearly, people
can be socially excluded, for example, because of poverty, and/or factors such as
age or disability, even if they live in prosperous communities.

How to 'measure' social exclusion has been the subject of a great deal of
academic debate. Most approaches have focused on people rather than
geographic areas and some have attempted to include measures that take
account of people's societal exclusion or isolation. It is not surprising that arts
practitioners did not feel it was appropriate to 'profile' and 'categorise' participants
in order to find out whether they met the criteria for 'socially excluded'.

> Everyone has different definitions of social exclusion. We call it a socially
> inclusive project, we don't use a different language to that which we use
> with participants. We're not qualified to make judgements about 'exclusion'
> and its criteria.
> Project partner

Targeting geographic areas and people

Some of the projects included in the research had targeted particular geographic
areas that experienced high levels of deprivation (as measured by deprivation
indices or identified by funders such as Single Regeneration Budget). This
approach often involved further targeting of people living within these areas. For
example City Arts and Angel Row Gallery worked in a community drop-in centre
and with a mental health group based in the Nottingham postcode district NG7,
and Artworks-mk and Milton Keynes Gallery targeted young people living on the
Coffee Hall estate, many of whom had been banned from a youth club (see
Appendix 1).

Other projects worked with organised groups or individuals who belonged to groups that were felt to experience exclusion. For example, the Mercury Theatre worked with young offenders and in HMP Channings Wood a writer in residence worked with a group of prisoners (see Appendix 1).

Inclusive practice

Some arts practitioners referred to projects being 'inclusive' but again, the term had different meanings. One referred to her project as 'inclusive' because it was open to everybody – she felt that only working with socially excluded groups was ghettoising. Another arts practitioner had developed what she referred to as inclusive practice; 'it involved identifying the practices that exclude people and eliminating those. It was never about thinking of certain people as excluded. I started to think about my practice as being an inclusive way of practising'. Her thinking led her to develop a project that took place within the Bull Ring market in Birmingham – it offered an inclusive space because it offered young people who might not attend youth groups arts access. 'Inclusive practice' also involved ensuring that the nature of facilitation and engagement were inclusive and prioritising the experiences and agenda of the participant (Hall, 2002). However, all practice in one way or another can perhaps be viewed as 'excluding'. For example, a project for young people effectively excludes older people.

3.4   The purpose of the arts

This research documented a range of arts projects that involved engaging individuals living in geographic areas that experience social exclusion or groups that were felt to experience social exclusion. However, we need to be clear that the work taking place can have many purposes. Some arts projects may attempt to specifically address problems related to social exclusion and thereby contribute to government targets, while others are not underpinned with such social objectives. For example, an arts project, rather than addressing 'health', might specifically work with a group of young women most at risk of unwanted pregnancy and, through a programme of information, advice and activities that develop confidence and awareness, enable those women to make more informed choices about birth control and pregnancy. Such a project would have measurable outcomes. However, an arts project could work with the same group and involve them in activities where there are no specific 'health' objectives.

> It depends utterly and completely on the point of the project, so each project has its clear purpose, has its clear objective, and if we're working

with a group of mental health users and one of the purposes is to enable them to articulate some of the issues that are concerning them, then that's the purpose of the project… but I do also believe passionately in just the process of participating in arts actually for its own sake, the sheer pleasure of being creative and discovering your own creative potential.
Project coordinator

A number of practitioners felt uncomfortable with the generalised claims that had been made about the arts and their ability to 'solve' social exclusion.

To be fair I think we can 'address' social exclusion but personally I don't think we can solve it, these are problems that are difficult to solve. There has been a certain amount of over-claiming and we ourselves are to blame for that.
Artist

A person who participates in a project will still have problems with housing, health, employment at the end of it – participating in an arts project is not magic that solves all. Also, the arts will only appeal to some people – others will have different interests.
Project partner

Some commentators, such as Merli (2000), have maintained that social exclusion can be removed only by fighting the structural conditions which cause it; such conditions will not be removed by benevolent arts programmes. Merli suggests that many intellectuals have started looking at society as a mere fact, 'they do not venture questions, hard criticism and struggle any more; they increasingly behave like "new missionaries", who play guitar with marginalised youth, the disabled and the unemployed, aiming at mitigating the perceptions which they have of their own exclusion'. She goes on to quote Kleinman (1998) who noted 'the current vogue is that … socially excluded areas don't just need jobs and better homes – apparently they need community centres, self-help groups, voluntary organisations and community businesses'.

Projects that contribute towards government targets

Unfortunately, the selection criteria used to choose organisations and projects for the research programme meant that relatively few of them were seeking *explicitly* to contribute towards government targets. Outcomes that might be of interest to those who have a social inclusion agenda, such as improved employability or a reduction in criminal behaviour, were felt by some organisations to be possible by-products of what they do, but they were not a key reason why the project took place. Some practitioners were of the belief that social exclusion *includes* exclusion from cultural opportunities. Projects that engaged people in cultural opportunities were then 'addressing' social exclusion.

Some case study projects were perhaps contributing more directly towards government goals than others. For example, *Fast Forward* aimed to engage young homeless people in a programme of outreach workshops and accredited training; *The Treatment* involved young people creating a play that tackled health issues; and *Vita Nova*, a theatre group for recovering addicts, has played an important role in people's ongoing recovery and the group deliver an extensive drug education programme in collaboration with Dorset Police (see Appendix 1).

Some of the projects highlighted the importance of considering the arts as part of a basket of measures to address problems. For example, the research included two arts projects happening in the context of the criminal justice system, but both the agency and artists steered away from drawing simplistic conclusions about projects reducing or stopping recidivism. For example, *Connections,* a project that involved prisoners reading excerpts from literature to help them understand their own behaviour, was not about confronting and actively challenging causations in terms of offending behaviour (see Appendix 1):

> We're looking at can you empathise with the text, can you relate to it in terms of your own relationships, can you think about this in terms of incidences in your own life?… We're not actually saying 'you, sorry I've just read your record and in 1993 you were up for assault'. That's not what it's about and I think that's fundamental.
> Tutor

Similarly, an interviewee from the North Essex Youth Offending Team, which collaborated with the Mercury Theatre in delivering a summer residency for young offenders, viewed the project as one of the tools in its armoury (see Appendix 1):

No one thing can stop a person offending but it gives them a real opportunity. It's about discipline, relationships, trust, building self-esteem… you're important and if you're not there, you let people down. It's probably the first time people have wanted them to be there. It turns some of their values on their heads.

Projects that offer cultural opportunities

Participatory arts
Most of the projects in the research involved creating opportunities for people to participate in arts activities – some of these projects had social and personal objectives such as to increase confidence and self-esteem. The opportunities offered were not merely offering 'access' to a cultural experience that was already there but involved participants actively engaging in and creating art.

Attendance at cultural venues
A few of the projects in the research had hoped to develop new audiences for the arts by enabling groups to attend venues. There were examples of projects – *Fashion and ID* and *Residence* – where participants engaged in participatory arts activities and were later encouraged to attend venues where their work was exhibited. However, there were two case study projects which did not have a participatory dimension. One of these, *Open House,* aimed to encourage participatory arts groups in Greater Manchester to attend museums, art galleries and theatres, while the other was a Unit for the Arts and Offenders project which offered training for artists wishing to work with vulnerable and volatile groups, and in criminal justice settings.

3.5 Summary

Allin (2000) has argued that it is not sufficient for an activity to be 'socially inclusive' simply by increasing access; the issue is whether or not such activities contribute to the outcomes of social inclusion and neighbourhood renewal. It is also the case that arts projects can occur in centres within socially excluded neighbourhoods, but may not tackle issues associated with social exclusion.

There are issues here for the Arts Council in being clear about language and the definitions it uses in dialogue within and outside the arts sector. What sort of work is of interest and what work is not? Is the Arts Council interested *only* in arts projects that explicitly 'tackle' social exclusion (eg crime, health, educational attainment etc), or is it interested in projects that offer socially excluded groups cultural opportunities and projects that might indirectly contribute to the outcomes of social inclusion?

4 Practice

This chapter explores principles and practice and considers some of the themes identified in the review (Jermyn, 2001) which were tested as part of the overarching research framework. Areas considered include: connecting with local needs; clearly stated aims and objectives; flexible and adaptable working methods; and quality. Partnership, sustainability and evaluation are considered in chapters 6-8.

4.1 Project initiation

The three Arts Council models

The research was originally set up to explore three models of arts practice:

- model 1 – community-led work, where the initiative for the arts project comes from a local community or group
- model 2 – experienced arts organisations or companies supported through the former Arts Council of England and Regional Arts Boards, for whom working with people from low income communities is a mainstay of their work
- model 3 – partnerships brokered by the Arts Council between established, regularly funded organisations with little or no experience of working with people and communities in low income areas and organisations with a track record of work in this field [16]

However, in practice it has proved difficult to allocate any of the projects explored in depth into the model 1 category. That is not to say these projects do not exist, because certainly arts organisations and practitioners had examples of projects initiated by local communities or groups. However, in each of the case studies, it was a Regional Arts Board, the Arts Council or an individual within an arts organisation that had initiated the project. In addition, although most were participatory arts projects or contained a participatory dimension, two did not fit this mould: *Open House* and *Training for Artists in the South East.*

The idea for setting up model 3 partnerships was part of the Arts Council's response to PAT 10. The original idea involved partnering an 'expert' organisation (ie an organisation for whom this area is the mainstay of their work) with a regularly funded organisation. The idea was later modified to recognise the need for some experience in the area, as the officer responsible for brokering the

---

[16] For a description of regularly funded organisations see footnote 1.

relationships explained: 'the regularly funded organisation would need to have willingness, commitment and some experience in the area and a confidence to take ideas further with people who really know what they're talking about'.

Four partnerships were brokered by the Arts Council:

- Artworks-mk and Milton Keynes Gallery
- Birmingham Opera and Optima Housing
- Cardboard Citizens and the RSC
- Eastern Touring Agency (now Momentum Arts) and Mercury Theatre

Connecting with local needs

Connecting with local needs was one of the 'good practice' principles identified in the literature review that informed the research (Jermyn, 2001). Unfortunately, the projects included in the Arts Council research did not include any that could be described as 'community-led'; a gap that could usefully be addressed in future research. Although none were initiated by communities themselves, practitioners often felt they were responding to a need (although one not necessarily articulated in formal terms by a group). There were, for example, cases of organisations delivering projects that built on 'pilot' projects or on previous work that had taken place in a particular community or with particular groups, of organisations developing projects with other agencies who had closer contact with a group (such as Youth Offending Teams), and of organisations using research to inform the development of a project proposal.

Many of the projects included in the research were funded through the Enabling Inclusion strand of the New Audiences Programme. Regional Arts Boards had solicited applications from organisations who had then submitted a project proposal describing the project they wished to undertake. At the proposal stage the basic structure of the project was outlined and it tended to be only after funding was agreed that organisations more formally consulted with groups and 'filled in the detail'.

The point made by some practitioners was that participants can find it difficult to make decisions about what they want unless they have had some prior exposure to the possibilities. This was one of the reasons that Magic Carpet delivered a series of taster sessions before seeking participants' views on what they would like to 'specialise' in; the tasters enabled people to make more informed decisions.

If more community-led projects had been included in the research it would have been useful to explore the nature of participants' involvement in arts projects, including their involvement in decision-making, using Arnstein's 'ladder of citizen participation' (Arnstein, 1971, cited in Russell, 1998). The ladder is a model that has informed discussions about the nature of people's involvement in community development but is a tool that has wider application. Arnstein identified eight levels of participation ranging from citizen control to manipulation:

1 citizen control
2 designated power
3 partnership
4 placation
5 consultation
6 information
7 therapy
8 manipulation

Some projects came to respond to people's needs as they developed. For example, *Vita Nova*, a theatre group for people in recovery from addiction to drugs, was created with a short-term aim – to create a good play. However, at the end of that process both the facilitator and the group wanted to continue, as the facilitator explained. 'It was a dual response. Had the play been rubbish and people hadn't been moved by it and the group had liked working together we might have had a weekly drama group or something. It was a combination of people wanting it to happen very badly.'

There was one interesting example where several components of what a project should consist of and how it should be delivered was imposed by an external agency. In practice, the delivering organisations had to abandon some of these ideas, in part because they did not match the needs of the communities they were working in. It illustrates the pitfalls of tailoring projects to meet the criteria of external agencies who do not necessarily have an in-depth knowledge of particular communities.

4.2   Clearly stated aims and objectives

Some commentators have identified 'clearly stated aims and objectives' as a good practice principle (see Chapter 2). Organisations participating in the research tended to set aims and objectives for all the projects they delivered.

However, a scan through the 15 case studies will reveal how much variation there is in the nature of objectives set by organisations. Some set objectives which could be reached relatively easily, while others set more challenging goals; some had objectives that focused on reaching certain numbers of people, some on achieving an end product (eg to create a play) and some on achieving outcomes (eg to raise confidence); some focused on the short term and others on the long term (eg to inspire an arts group to continue). This has implications in terms of judging the success or failure of projects purely on whether they meet their stated aims and objectives – one would not be comparing like with like.

But why set objectives at all? Most felt having aims and objectives vital in terms of having and keeping a clear focus and that the process of setting objectives was beneficial.

> If we're not clear about what we want to achieve we ain't going to achieve it. We're clearly saying, 'we're going to have a play at the end of this and you're going to contribute to it, you're going to help devise it, you're going to get up and do it'. By setting those parameters and succeeding, you magnify the achievement.
> Director/facilitator

> Generally, yes, we set aims and objectives for projects, it's down in black and white here, you have to do that or it's a chicken without a head.
> Project coordinator

There were examples of some practitioners who had not written down aims and objectives at the start of the project but knew what it was they were setting out to do and formalised aims and objectives at a later stage. In one case, Bournemouth Theatre in Education, the facilitator could not have anticipated what the eventual aims of *Vita Nova* would be (see Appendix 1). Two of the model 3 partnerships set aims and objectives, one preferred to work organically (although set objectives for some aspects of the project) and another had no aims beyond making a good show.

The point was made that many objectives could be met in a fairly superficial way but the integrity of artists and arts organisations was such that they genuinely wanted to do more than achieve objectives 'on paper' and avoid pursuing objectives 'at all costs'.

One of the things I admired about ___, was at one point he could have forced it with the older people because they are quite anxious to please. So we had to be careful not to manipulate that. So at one point he could very easily have said 'okay, here's the camera, do it'. Not quite in that way, but put pressure on them or he could have taken photographs of them when actually they would have been giving their consent but under obligation... We did ask one another quite seriously when we met is this going to be a real project or not? Because we could have gone that route.
Artist

It depends how effective you want it to be and how many numbers you want to be affected, or how much of an impact you want to have. I could have just gone in and delivered workshops, fairly poor workshops, and get some people in, 'they're free so don't moan'. I could have met the objectives on paper but surely to be socially included in something – that takes time, it takes time.
Project coordinator

There were some cases of aims and objectives being set which, on reflection, organisations felt were unrealistic and where the practicalities of 'how do we achieve this?' were not thought through.

[reflecting on a skills exchange objective] There was always had an element of pie in the sky about it. I never quite saw, even under the best of circumstances, where the skills exchange was going to come from. Unless we had worked in a totally integrated way, how skills were going to be exchanged, apart from in a very superficial way.
Project partner

[reflecting on an objective where a specified percentage audience target was set] ... some of the aims and objectives, I look at them now and I think why did we put that in? And I think again, part of it was the time and the need to get this thing done quickly... But I think now we're much better educated as an organisation and we would sit down and say are these reasonable aims and objectives, how are we going to measure these targets, are we setting too many objectives?
Project partner

> Perhaps we didn't set out to tackle these [aims] as well as we might. These are huge aims, perhaps we needed to be a bit more realistic or have more specific aims.
> Project partner

One difficulty, particularly if the project involved trying something new, was knowing whether something was achievable or not. For example, one artist noted that she found setting targets difficult, particularly when there was no benchmark and she was yet to meet the people she would be working with:

> The only thing that has been difficult is setting targets… until we actually get out and talk to people and get started and see who's going to be engaged by the things we're doing and who will we pick up as a result of that engagement, we felt a little uneasy about setting the targets. Even though everyone has been very kind about it and said 'look it doesn't matter, you just have to say the numbers and they're almost arbitrary' in a sense it doesn't feel like that when you're setting them.
> Artist

Some projects felt they needed more time to meet their aims. For example, one aim of *Fashion and ID* was that older and younger people living on the same housing estate would work together, while *eState of the Art* hoped that young people from different estates and different towns would meet to exchange ideas and experiences. Both were examples of projects where the arts practitioners involved felt it would have been inappropriate to bring the different groups together simply in order to 'tick a box'; it was a process that needed to be handled sensitively and required a longer timeframe than was available.

Partnership projects raised the issue of organisations having different understandings of objectives. In two cases, objectives were set and agreed but it became apparent as the projects developed that the parties had interpreted the objectives in different ways. In both cases the partnerships involved one agency that was very experienced working in a social exclusion context and one agency which had comparatively less experience, and there was confusion over which group was to be targeted.

4.3   Recruiting artists and participants

Internal or external artist?

The medium-scale agencies participating in the research programme, such as Darts, Jubilee Arts, Soft Touch and Community Music East, had a core team of paid staff and contracted workers who delivered or facilitated arts activity. However, many organisations hired freelance artists on a project-by-project basis and this raised a number of issues such as:

- finding and recruiting artists with the necessary skills
- setting up a successful working structure in which freelance artists and organisations could work
- ensuring there was an adequate support structure for freelance artists working with vulnerable groups
- ensuring artists were briefed about the policies, principles, ways of working etc

Some established organisations had formalised procedures and policies to support and protect artists and participants (eg formalised codes of practice, rules about 'acceptable behaviour', risk assessment procedures etc) but others did not. All artists and arts organisations should adopt good practice principles in protecting vulnerable participants and the artists working with them but the research suggests that organisations did not share information, and that procedures and policies developed in a more ad hoc way.

During the latter stages of the research the events of Soham were unfolding. This may have led to a heightened awareness of child protection issues and the measures that should be taken to protect children and young people - certainly some interviewees referred to their organisation as being more aware.[17]

---

[17] During the research period the Arts Council published *Keeping Arts Safe* (Arts Council, 2003) which provides guidance on child protection issues and on devising policies and procedures to protect children, young people and vulnerable adults involved in arts activities. Although very relevant to social inclusion work, it would be useful to consider whether there are additional safety issues that are relevant to artists and arts organisations working in social exclusion contexts that should be considered.

Recruitment of participants

A further good practice principle identified through the review (Jermyn, 2001), and forming part of the research framework, was the need to devise appropriate participant recruitment strategies. Some projects involved artists going to work with groups on their own territory, while some used outreach and then introduced people to new settings. The recruitment methods used depended on the setting and the group but artists often stressed the importance of making face-to-face contact as part of the recruitment process.

The early stages of projects often involved building trust, hence the importance placed on outreach.

> The outreach was about going into their environment and building up trust. You have to build up that relationship. If they didn't know us and we said come to a new place, well when there's so much going on in their lives it just wouldn't work.
> Artist

> It's building trust. You know what I was saying about 'we want this', if you go in with that attitude I don't think people would come back. It was so directed that it didn't allow people to have an input. You don't want to alienate people.
> Artist

> It has been very much a changing role. To begin with, it was about a lot of things. It was about working with a very low baseline of skills and building those up, getting them to stand up straight and speak out. It was about gaining trust from them so that I could tell their stories, so that they could share their stories with me.
> Director/facilitator

Some projects took place in unfamiliar settings from the outset but the artist or facilitator had often met potential participants on neutral ground or in participants' own environment before the project began. For example, the director/facilitator at Bournemouth Theatre in Education went to visit potential participants in their recovery centre rather than just inviting them to meet her at the community centre where rehearsals would be taking place.

For some participants, going to an unfamiliar setting was a big step and needed to be handled with sensitivity. For example, *Fast Forward* provided young homeless people with access to outreach in hostels, shelters and temporary accommodation before introducing them to more structured sessions held at Fusion's base in a community centre.

4.4   Project delivery

Models of participation

Some projects could be categorised as outreach and others took place in settings that were unfamiliar to participants; but in both settings projects often culminated in a performance, exhibition or sharing of work. The 'sharings' were viewed by arts practitioners as a way of celebrating and sharing people's achievements and the interviews with participants showed how these events played an important role in enhancing their feeling of pride (see Chapter 5).

> There was a time when I would have said it doesn't matter about the product, it's all about the process, but I think the idea of product drives the process. Without the end, without working toward some event or sharing people lose interest – it's some strange human condition thing that we like to show what we've done – it's a kind of ritual.
> Director/facilitator

> The main reason [for holding an event] is a mark of respect for the people that have been involved and the amount of effort they've put in. As I said, I realised quite a long time ago that you can't just ask people to do good work and then not distribute it properly… Whereas if we just base all our work on the process, which when community arts first started it was very much more process-based, the idea of making products to distribute or even worse, to sell, that was wrong. It all had to be based around what people did in the session.
> Artist

Democratic structures

Issues such as shared control and collaborative working have previously been identified as contributory success factors, therefore one of the subjects explored in the research framework was the relationship between the artist and participants. The social inclusion work included in the Arts Council research often

41

had some level of democratic ethos, but that is not to say that participants controlled the agenda or that an 'anything goes' attitude was evident. The survey of 31 participants showed that 29 of them felt they had had freedom to develop their ideas, 26 felt that the artists had been interested in what participants thought, 24 felt that they had been challenged to try new things and think in a different way and 16 felt they had had a say over what happened in sessions. It is interesting to consider how issues such as collaborative working, control and ownership were evident across the different artforms.

Literature
Connections used what the facilitator referred to as a 'democratic forum' in which staff facilitated discussions with prisoners about literature. There were no right or wrong answers – everyone's view was valid – but the discussions were still facilitated by staff.

> They sorted that out [the dynamics of the group] pretty well. They got people talking in turn, to say their part.
> Participant

> I think the staff were great but ___ especially, has a great knack in bringing it back on track. When I say bringing it on track I don't mean restricting it but keeping it together and feeding insight rather than directing – asking really important questions.
> Participant

> They [the facilitators] led the way by talking about how their own personal experience related to characters in the first two or three short stories we read. Then one or two people carried on and I suppose that was the inspiration if you like – that's what we're here for.
> Participant

Drama
Within the drama projects, participants were involved in a devising process in which material was generated from their ideas, improvisation and exercises. Often participants felt a strong sense of ownership of what was produced but the process was led by a director/facilitator.

> The balance is, I am throughout the process looking to generate material that's going to be able to be turned into a decent play so in that sense I'm running it. However, what we're trying to gain through the process is

content of material that relates to those young people's experience or interest. There are those who would say 'no it should be a democratic process, it should be all the ideas of the young people themselves and nothing else, and done the way they want to do it'. That way you don't end up with a piece of art or, rather, you're unlikely to, because it won't be structured because they won't have the skills to do it necessarily.
Director/facilitator

The structure, I've observed and been to projects where they can do what they like, kids make what they want, but my feeling is that's too difficult. It's too wide, sometimes what you see is a lot of people sitting around not doing anything.
Director/facilitator

In the Mercury Theatre's summer residency for young offenders participants worked alongside two professional actors. This was in some senses a very democratic way of working in that there was an equitable relationship between the professional actors and participants – all were members of the cast in a project which was being led by an artistic director.

Visual arts and digital arts
Within the visual arts, artists would often provide some kind of structure or format but allowed participants freedom within that to make choices. For example, participants in *Fashion and ID* created life-size silhouettes of themselves and within the outline created a collage. While prescriptive in one sense, there was also lots of freedom and some chose to break the perimeters set by artists; for example, one participant did not want the shape of her body portrayed so she did an alien figure with words on it while others wanted their profiles exaggerated so they looked muscle-bound.

It's actually giving them a format into which to have that freedom, a place of safety really... It's not good enough as an artist to just give them the materials and say 'there you go, you're so wonderfully creative, how lovely'. That isn't actually working with people.
Artist

Very often I will already know what I want that person to produce and what I'm doing is leading them down that path so they come to that point ... A lot of it's down to your own personal integrity, you have to believe in it, that it's more important to get their ideas than something that might be better

43

than they could come up with… it's got to come from them. My job is to give them examples of ways, that will expand, develop their ideas, rather than inflict my values on them.
Artist

We're very fussy about the artists we use, we wouldn't have an artist design a mural and say 'now you paint that' – that's using the young people as factory workers I think. Every element of it has been a creative, collaborative process.
Project partner

Flexible working methods

How flexibility operates within arts projects involving socially excluded groups was one of the subjects explored through the research; the importance of flexibility was a recurring theme in interviews and was evident in many different ways. Artists spoke of the importance of reading the mood of the group, or of individuals on the day, and responding appropriately.

I try to create the conditions in which people can work successfully. It's relaxed but there is a focus. You have to assess the conditions of people at any given point in the day. If somebody comes in the morning in a particular condition, for whatever reason… You have to have different ways of coming up with stuff. It's absolutely fundamental and crucial, that right from the word go you engage with the people you're working with.
Director/facilitator

… it's also important to be aware when somebody is going through a bad time. You can pick up on things I think – if you know somebody and they're feeling under pressure or there are other things going on.
Artist

Arts practitioners found ways of meeting individuals' needs and accommodating their particular interests or strengths. There was an agenda or end goal but the process retained a level of flexibility; as one artist put it, 'you know where you are going but there may be different ways of getting there'.

We have a weekly review of what's happened and we can change the direction or move it so we keep them [participants] on board. What we

wouldn't do is have an idea at the beginning and slavishly follow that idea and direct towards that end point.
Artist

For example, Soft Touch worked with Verve, a group of people with physical, sensory and learning disabilities and the end goal was to create a website. The individuals in the group had different personalities, abilities and interests and the artists worked flexibly to include everyone. Similarly, in *Residence* the artists got around barriers people had about writing, by transcribing what people had to say, playing word association games, making use of magnetic letters and using letter stamps. Projects sometimes involved working with people who could not physically use certain pieces of equipment themselves, so artists adapted their methods as appropriate eg participants would direct the artist or collaborate with the artist to achieve the task.

> The bit I enjoyed the most was working on the cartoons. I can't draw or write so I had to visualise it and tell him [the worker]. He sat with me to do this [the cartoon strip]. I explained what I wanted and he did it. He does what I explain – so plane, holiday!
> Participant

Projects were paced to suit the needs of participants. Indeed, in some situations this created a certain amount of tension eg when there was a 'fixed' slot for exhibiting work in a gallery.

> There's also need in terms of the paces people work at. The level of support they might need in producing work differs. Some people like to be more independent, like this morning in the darkroom. Some people like more guidance than others, while some like to be left to it.
> Artist

A number of projects accommodated people's practical needs (providing transport to venues, providing a creche for childcare, providing food). Two of the case study projects had to draft in additional staff after projects had started; this kind of flexibility required additional financial resources to be found.

Artist-to-participant ratios

Successful projects often involved artists working with relatively small numbers of people. The smallest groups had only two or three participants and the ratio of participants to artists was one-to-one. Others worked with larger groups but the importance of offering people one-to-one attention was a recurrent theme.

> For a start there's two tutors there, so if somebody is struggling with something you've got one tutor who's addressing the group and it's possible to be also offering a one-to-one in that situation as well. So if somebody's struggling then there could be a tutor being next to them specifically working with them, while the needs of the group are always being addressed.
> Tutor

> … certain participants need more one-to-one and guidance, and there are so many varying needs within the group that I think you have to be flexible and work with the individual.
> Artist

> Everybody tried to include people. They've been incredibly sensitive and brought in humour which is always good! It's been very inclusive and involved everyone at different levels. It's been pitched just right.
> Worker from participating group

> There were a range of skills and abilities. We have the techniques but again there has to be a lot of adaptation, working one-to-one.
> Artist

Quality

The research framework identified pride in achievement and quality as factors that contributed to a successful outcome (see Chapter 2). In the research, artists said 'quality' had relevance to projects, not only in terms of process but also final output, and were able to articulate how this was related to pride in achievement.

> There has to be two strands to it. There's the quality in the relationship you form with the group. The quality in all those kinds of things we're aiming for like self-esteem and respect and all that type of stuff. But also quality. If you are making a play, I feel there has to be quality to that. And actually a

lot of those things like self-esteem come out of feeling that you've done something that's good, and strong and works… I feel that it's the facilitator's job to ensure that quality and push for it, demand it to a certain extent.
Director/facilitator

There was a belief among artists that the better the final result, the greater participants' sense of achievement.

I think there has to be quality, it's another word which is very difficult, but the work has to be of high quality. And not just the quality of the produced work, but quality of the intention has to be high as well… Because that's what people deserve and why bother doing anything else? There's absolutely no point. As __ said, they say 'actually I think I could do this better' or 'I am not pleased with this result'.
Artist

It's a less valuable achievement if what they produce at the end, people come along to see it and say 'jolly good, well done, you put something together'. I think if what they put together is presented with a level of professional skill and presentation elements, people come and go 'that is fantastic', then you're in a different ball game. My criteria if you like, is that I'm striving to ensure that the quality of what they produce at the end is no less good than any other community group, or amateur theatre group or any other work that happens in this theatre because anything less is patronising. It's to do with the expectations that people have had of them – low expectations, you have to have high expectations.
Director/facilitator

In visual arts projects, quality was evident in the way work was finished and exhibited. There was a belief that participants' work should be presented in a way that showed it to its best. For example, participants in *Thorntree Glitter* produced items of jewellery that were exhibited in a professionally curated exhibition at Cleveland Craft Centre, while participants in Fusion's project had their work shown in a community centre but it was nevertheless presented in a professional way. In drama, the focus was on achieving as professional a performance as possible. Emphasis was placed on rehearsal, on tightening up the start and end of scenes, on getting details right.

One practitioner noted that for her, quality was not something that was fixed, and which we all know and recognise as the same thing. For her, quality was about working with an individual and identifying what quality it is that they were aspiring to, and working with them to achieve that.

4.5   Summary

The research highlighted the importance of the following:

- building in time to plan and research projects. For example, time was needed to develop appropriate recruitment strategies and lay the foundations for successful partnership working
- setting clear and realistic aims and objectives that are worked through in terms of delivery and understood by all partners, including the artists responsible for leading arts activity. If those aims and objectives are to be used as a tool for monitoring and developing projects then they need to be revisited while the project is in progress (not just looked at when projects end)
- supporting people's participation by meeting their practical needs (covering people's travel costs, providing a creche, supplying food or food vouchers and so on)
- having flexible and adaptable working methods (but retaining a clear vision nevertheless)
- working collaboratively with participants – all projects had a democratic dimension but an 'anything goes' approach was not evident, indeed some of the activity was strongly led or directed
- pursuing quality – both in the process and outcome
- responding to individuals' needs – this may have implications in terms of needing more than one artist leading activity or costing in the support of someone with specialist skills, such as a youth worker, for example. The importance of giving participants one-to-one attention was a recurrent theme
- adopting procedures and policies that protect artists and participants
- creating a working structure that allows freelance artists and organisations to work together effectively

5   Outcomes

As discussed in Chapter 2 and in Appendix 2, a wide range of claims have been made about the impact of the arts. The research was not an 'impact study' but, because it sought to explore measures of success and explore the characteristics of successful (and not so successful) initiatives, some exploration of outcomes was necessary. The researcher interviewed artists and project coordinators about the outcomes of projects and, where possible, interviewed participants. This chapter provides an overview of the impact of participation on participants and draws largely on material collected in interviews with participants. Readers with an interest in individual project outcomes should refer to the case studies which appear in Appendix 1.

5.1   Methods

As noted in chapter 4, very few of the case study projects were tackling *explicitly* the problems associated with social exclusion, although they did involve working with socially excluded groups or in socially excluded communities. Participants were generally participating in projects that involved attending workshops over a period of weeks or months, rather than large-scale, community-led arts programmes (see Table 1, Chapter 1, for further information).

As part of the Arts Council research, a participant survey was administered at the end of projects. Thirty-one participants were interviewed using the questionnaire although, in some instances, it had to be tailored to fit the interview situation. For example, not all questions were asked if time was particularly limited or if participants' needs were such that a more discursive approach was appropriate.[18] The 31 respondents were drawn from seven projects: Bournemouth Theatre in Education; City Arts and Angel Row Gallery; *Connections*; ETA and Mercury Theatre; Fusion; Horn Reflections; and Soft Touch.[19] Twenty-one of the respondents were male and the most common age categories were 16-20 (13 respondents) and 25-54 (13 respondents). In addition, 22 other participants and nine group coordinators or leaders were interviewed (see Chapter 2).

Because of the Arts Council's desire to explore an indicator-based research approach, the questionnaire contained a number of statements with which people

---

[18] As noted in Chapter 2, originally a before-and-after research approach had been envisaged but this proved to be impractical.

[19] Chapter 1 and the case studies in Appendix D describe these projects in more detail.

could agree or disagree. This enabled certain outcomes to be quantified. The questionnaire also contained a number of open-ended questions which provided the researcher with an opportunity to explore certain areas of inquiry in more detail. For example, participants were asked if they felt proud of what they had achieved on the project and were provided with 'yes', 'not really' and 'don't know' response categories. Those that indicated yes or not really were then asked to expand on their answer. Also, there were less structured discussions that arose from people giving certain answers. For example, participants were asked how much they had enjoyed doing the project and provided with various categories of response. What often followed on from that was a discussion about what they had enjoyed and why. The data that emerged from the interviews were rich in qualitative detail but the sample was small so caution in generalising findings to a wider population is advised.

The research raised some ethical issues. Although the purpose of the research was clearly explained in simple terms, it is difficult to know the extent to which interviewees truly understood the explanations given.[20] Protecting the anonymity of respondents was also a concern; no names have been used in this report and care has been taken in writing up the research to protect identities. However, many projects had only small numbers of participants and the outcomes were very public (eg a website, a performance). There was also a need to conduct interviews in a sensitive way; people sometimes shared information of a very personal nature, sometimes outside the context of a formal interview (over the course of a cigarette break, for example). As a result of some of these issues, the researcher has withheld some information from the report because she judged it inappropriate to use the material in this way. However, the information informs the research nevertheless.

Further, in the context of the arts projects included in the research there was an issue about the extent to which the researcher should 'intrude' into that environment and make demands of participants (which would usually take them away from arts time) – it was not only a practical issue but an ethical one. For example, in the interests of research it might have been desirable to have administered a baseline questionnaire at the start of all projects and tests to provide scientific measures of participants' self-esteem. However, the start of

---

[20] For example, an explanation was provided at the start of one interview and the respondent seemed to understand but at the end the interviewee asked the researcher if she was a journalist and would be writing something for the newspaper. The local newspaper had previously run a feature on the project so the interviewee was more familiar with this form of interviewing and reporting.

projects was often a delicate time where participants were yet to fully engage with projects and it would have been very inappropriate in some contexts for an external researcher to go in to projects and take this approach.[21] The relationship between the researcher and participants benefited from having time to develop - participants became used to the researcher's presence, rapport and trust was built up, there was a shared knowledge of certain events and so on. To have made demands from the start would potentially have compromised the relationship and, in the end, the quality of the resulting data.

5.2   Increase in arts skills and appreciation

Twenty-eight participants were asked how much experience they had had of the arts in general in the last two years; half felt they had had 'little' or 'no' experience and half had had 'a lot' or 'fair amount' of experience. Participants were also asked how much experience they had had of the project artform – 10 indicated they had little or no experience but 18 had had a lot or fair amount of experience. Younger participants were most likely to indicate that they had recent experience of the project artform, either at school or at college. Nine of the 28 participants said they had done a project like it in the past (the last two years was given as a time-frame).

Approximately half of participants (12 of 25 participants) said they had changed their views about the arts as a result of participating in the project. Five had changed their views 'a lot' and seven 'a little'. Each described feeling more positive about arts or having more developed views. However, participants when describing how they felt about the arts before projects started tended to speak about them in a positive way – most were already positively predisposed to them and none held what could be described as 'negative' views.

> My views are more developed, more evolved.
> Participant

> Before this I thought theatre was like second grade cinema but I've come to respect it, the performing arts.
> Participant

---

[21] There would also be practical difficulties carrying out this approach in projects that had a shifting population. An alternative approach would have been for artists to interview participants at the start or to make baseline assessments, but again this would have been problematic as artists may well not have the skills, time or feel it appropriate to take this route.

It's opened my eyes to some different areas that I've never been involved in before. How can I put it? I've never been near that kind of environment for learning so that's changed my views on that a little bit. It's changed my views on the way you can learn. It's broadened my horizons.
Participant

My views haven't changed because I love the arts but my understanding and my appreciation of literature have increased. It's more about the actual way you can use it - that's what's changed. It's usefulness, the using it.
Participant

I've discovered talents for things I never knew were there.
Participant

Almost all participants felt they had learned new skills. Out of 29 participants, three felt they had developed 'lots' of skills, 22 had developed 'some' skills, three felt they had learned no new skills and one did not know. Often the skills participants referred to were arts skills. For example, young people participating in Horn Reflections' drama project felt they had learned new things about creating characters, structuring a play and writing.

Definitely [have learned new skills]. I've never wrote poems before but I wrote a good poem
Participant

All participants agreed with the statement 'I feel I have developed a better appreciation of the artform' as a result of participating in the project and many intended to continue being involved in the artform in the future. For example, participants on *Connections* had read books before taking the course but often their reading had been restricted to a particular genre, such as thrillers or horror, or books that supported their studies (see Appendix 1). As a result of the course, participants found they read in a different way and were happy to read a wider range and different types of books.

It's changed me a little bit…To the point of liking different types of literature that I otherwise wouldn't have even tried. I wouldn't have gone near them – not a chance… It's changing the stuff that I'm reading now.
Participant

All participants felt they had been creative and used their imaginations. Project outputs included the artwork itself which included books, boxes customised with words and metal work, collages, items of jewellery, mosaics, music, murals, plays, poetry, sculptural structures, textiles and websites.

5.3   Increased self-confidence

Research studies have frequently identified an increase in self-confidence as an outcome of arts participation. For example, Matarasso's (1997) survey of 243 adults participating in arts programmes established that 84% of participants felt more confident about what they could do. Commentators have noted that raised self-confidence in individuals can manifest itself in different ways. For example, Hill and Moriarty's (2001) report about the Merseyside ACME Access and Participation programme noted the results of increases in confidence and self-esteem included individuals using arts projects as a stepping stone into pre-vocational education or into employment. [22] The authors noted local people gave considerable voluntary time and energy to managing and organising arts projects and that participation in arts activities 'seemed to support an attitude of "what's next?" in individuals, which encouraged both personal development and wider involvement in their local community'. Dewson et al (2000), who designed a model for measuring increases in employability or 'distance travelled' for projects operating under European Social Fund Objective 3, noted how the acquisition of certain soft outcomes, such as confidence, can represent an immense leap forward for some individuals.

In the Arts Council study, participants were asked if the project had changed the way they thought about themselves and what they could do; in almost all cases the answer was 'yes'. Often participants described how projects had boosted their confidence. For some, the increase in confidence had been small and for others it was more significant.

> … I wasn't worth a damn, there was no purpose to my life… a year ago I couldn't have talked to you, I didn't talk to anybody… What has helped me, it has helped me build self-esteem and confidence.
> Participant

---

[22] The programme encouraged and supported over 120 arts-led community regeneration projects.

I've developed confidence in myself and my abilities. It was a long process of getting up every morning, turning up, taking part over a long period of time.
Participant

I don't feel 'oh yeah, I feel great now I've finished the *Connections* course', but I do feel a bit more confident. Like I feel more confident speaking to you telling you what I did just now. I've got a little more perspective on other people's views perhaps.
Participant

We cannot draw conclusions from the evidence about the extent to which increases in confidence transferred to other areas of people's lives or whether increases were long-lasting. However, some of the participants indicated that this had happened in their case.

It's given me confidence in terms of my self, there was a time I didn't have any faith [in the project]… My confidence has gone up there and I'm ready to take on the world! … I've got involved in running a project – doing this has given me confidence in what can be done.
Participant

Doing this has helped me be more confident with people. I think I have surprised myself, I can do this and I've got something to give people and have the nerve it takes to face people.
Participant

I got up on stage and acted in front of people… It's made me more confident, more aware I can do things if I put my mind to it. It's made me try other things as well. Even talking to people, it's made me more confident talking to people, not to be afraid I think. I might try and see whether I can go to a drama group, I would never have done that before.
Participant

5.4   Sense of well being

The HDA (2000) review, *Arts for health: a review of good practice in community-based arts projects and initiatives which impact on health and well being*, concerned itself with arts projects aimed at community participation, capacity building and regeneration, as well as those with health or health promotion objectives. The authors suggested there was more evidence (albeit anecdotal), as well as a stronger indication that increased well being and self-esteem was directly related to involvement with the art and not just with socialising or carrying out the physical activity involved. In the HDA case studies, improvements in well being were commonly reported by projects to include enhanced motivation, greater connectedness to others, having a more positive outlook on life and a reduced sense of fear, isolation or anxiety. Further, such benefits were often brought about by the opportunities that engagement in art afforded for self-expression, enhanced sense of value and attainment, and pride in achievement.

Matarasso (1997) concluded 'it was clear people derived great pleasure from being involved in arts activities and it added greatly to their quality of life'. He proposed that improved health and well being was one of the outcomes of arts participation; this outcome was indicated by people 'feeling better or healthier' or 'feeling happier'.[23]

In the Arts Council research, over half of participants agreed with the statement 'being involved in this project has helped me feel good about myself' (16 out of 23 people). Fewer felt that projects had helped them feel 'better or healthier' (10 out of 23 people). It is perhaps not surprising that when participants completed something they were pleased with and which was valued by others, they felt good about themselves. However, it is worth remembering that some participants described in interviews how they had previously had very low levels of self-esteem and how the arts had made a significant contribution to raising their esteem levels. For other participants, participation in projects had given them 'a bit of a lift'.

> In a bad situation doing something like that [*Connections*] makes you have a better outlook, you're achieving something. So you're thinking I'm in here [prison] but at least I'm getting somewhere.
> Participant

> It was something to get up for in the morning, something to look forward to.
> Participant

---

[23] 52% of participants said they felt better and 73% said they felt happier since being involved. However, this is one area of Matarasso's work which has been criticised by Belfiore (2002) who suggests that attempting to measure quantitatively something so subjective, requires more in-depth discussion and a more complex investigation of participants' experiences than Matarasso provides.

> In terms of my life I love it. Even on bad days it makes me feel better. It's relaxing in my mind, everything on the outside world is on the outside. It reinforces there is more to life than just the bad stuff… if I go through a bad patch they help me and I'm not on my own.
> Participant

> [The play] It takes your mind out of prison and you can go back and think about it. I mean, there were people talking about it for about a week afterwards and they weren't even on the course! People that went, who didn't even know what they were looking at to be quite honest… I think that [*Macbeth*] was very valuable.
> Participant

Most participants felt that the projects had broadened their horizons (21 out of 23 participants) and fewer that it had improved their quality of life (15 out of 23 participants).

5.5   Pride and fulfilment

Personal pride

Almost all participants interviewed felt proud of what they had achieved (27 out of 31 participants). Participants were also asked to choose words that best described how they felt at the end of projects from a grid of words – proud was the most commonly selected word (12 participants) followed by inspired (11 participants).

All the participants had completed tasks and seen things through until the end – they were all interviewed at the end of projects. Regularly attending a project and completing something was, for some, a source of pride in itself. For example, one participant never finished anything, he had a history of not seeing things through but he was proud of having regularly attended rehearsals and seeing the project through to its conclusion.

> I'm quite chuffed I finished the course. And now I've seen their report on me I'm quite pleased with that too – it's a good report.
> Participant

I'm proud that I've done it and saw it through… It felt like a long journey but I was proud in the end. In September, there were just three of us in a room. From nothing we created something.
Participant

Individuals also derived a great deal of pride from the fact that the things they created, whether it be a piece of theatre, a page for a website, or an item of jewellery, were *theirs*. This sense of ownership had been supported through a collaborative creative process (see Chapter 4).

They're *my* ideas. There's a white background with a red circle on and there's writing through it. It's like the Japanese flag. I like bright colours, metallic colours.
Participant

I feel proud I created a character and performed it and I had the audience's attention.
Participant

The detail and everything was exactly how the children had drawn it, so it was their work, it hadn't been altered in any way…. She [the artist] hadn't thought, 'that's a bit thin I'll just widen it a little bit', everything was done exactly to what the drawings were. My daughter had done cufflinks, she was only seven at the time so obviously her drawings weren't going to be fantastic, but they were *her* drawings and that's how they came out and nothing was changed. It was exactly how she drew it in the first place which I thought was lovely.
Participant

[Is proud of] The stories, everything, came out of heads. Each of us contributed to the story… When we were rehearsing we improvised because nothing was written and ___ [the tutor] wrote [up] the script. It came out of our heads and then she wrote things into proper English.
Participant

Having your work shown to others and valued by them also generated feelings of pride. In drama, the reaction and applause of the audience was one of the measures used by both facilitator/directors and participants to judge how good the play and performance had been. In exhibitions, people derived pride from seeing their work professionally presented in a public exhibition.

I surprised myself. People who saw this play said you've really improved because this play was more professional than the one before... People told me I'm a good actor... it makes me feel good about myself, it makes me feel proud.
Participant

The feeling after I've done a really good performance and I know it and I'm feeling on top of the world and the audience is applauding.
Participant

To think people will be looking at my work [on the web]. Fantastic!
Participant

Doing the play. It was puckka in front of the audience. At the time I was thinking I'll have a laugh and bunk off today but I didn't. It went perfectly.
Participant

In *Connections*, a course in which prisoners used literature to reflect on their behaviour, several participants were proud of having talked about their feelings within the group.

... because a lot of stuff I talked about... I wouldn't even talk about it to a friend.
Participant

I feel proud that I found myself in a group environment with people I hadn't had any contact with and was still able to express myself and talk about internal issues.
Participant

Group pride

Participants were also proud of what the group as a whole had achieved (26 of 31 participants). Within groups everyone had made a contribution – an outcome that had been supported through the arts process, which had placed an emphasis on working flexibly to include everyone and providing one-to-one attention.

The most positive thing about the course was the change within the group itself. Day one people were very, very apprehensive and suspicious of the fact there was an officer there [prison officer]. They were concerned of what the motives behind it were. As the group went on over the ten weeks or so you saw people relaxing and trusting the rest of the group and feeling they could speak more openly.
Participant

I was pleased with *everybody's* result not just mine. Everybody's put work into it and tried their best. When you see it on the screen it will be fantastic – bright and colourful. I want to know what it comes out like. That's the best part of it. I think it's going to look good.
Participant

I feel proud of what the group achieved. There was a lot of people there and… they've been through a lot and probably been some of the nastiest people you could meet, they've hit personal lows and to be able to sit and talk about that, and realise what they had actually come to themselves, and to be sat there and stick with it for the ten weeks… you have to feel proud of them haven't you?
Participant

We all helped each other which is really good – that's what it's like isn't it? We've not worked as a group like that before. I think it's the best project I've been involved in. I reckon it's been very interesting for everyone.
Participant

There were examples of group workers successfully using arts projects to contribute to their own agendas. For example, one wanted a group that had been established for some time to start working in a different way – she felt participation in the project had changed members' perception of what the group was about, had got them working together and improved their confidence and self-esteem.

5.6   Social contact and social skills

Many people had made new friends through arts projects (16 out of 30 people) and, in almost all cases, people felt 'very' or 'fairly likely' they would stay friends with them after the project. Those that had not made new friends tended to be those participants who were part of a pre-existing group (so knew everyone anyway) or were participating in the prison-based project (so they knew their fellow inmates or preferred to think of fellow participants as 'associates' rather than friends). For some, meeting people and making friends had been one of the things people had enjoyed the most.

> The people, the people were bloody amazing. They're probably the nicest people I've ever met.
> Participant

Regularly attending workshops in some instances was felt by some artists to be an indicator of self-development and confidence in social settings. For example, some of the homeless people participating in Fusion's *Fast Forward* project had very unstable and chaotic lives. One of the artists delivering the project noted, 'it was a challenge for some participants even to leave their rooms, let alone participate consistently and creatively in group activities'.

Participants generally felt they had worked as part of a team (24 of 31 people). The feeling of being part of a team was particularly strong in theatre projects where participants worked collaboratively to achieve a shared goal – the performance. The work involved trust, cooperation, listening and putting across their own ideas.

> I think when you're working to the same objective you forget about your background and anything else because you're all focused. You're all in the same position, you've all got nerves and that makes you quite a solid group, a more emphatic group because you've all got the same problems and the same goals, you all want to do well... you don't want to let each other down.
> Participant

> I liked the way we helped each other – people had a spread of skills, some in writing, some in acting and everyone contributed to the play... You had to prove what you were good at – some were good at comedy or whatever.
> Participant

Other projects had a joint goal but involved a substantial amount of independent working. For example, participants in one project created their own web pages to feed into a larger group website. In other projects the end goal was in some ways quite individual. For example, families participating in *Thorntree Glitter* designed and produced items of jewellery but the work had taken place in a very social and collaborative environment and the process ended with an exhibition:

> Participant 1: Because everybody helped each other as well, if anyone was stuck it was 'I'll cut that up for you', because some couldn't use the scissors for the bags (used to make garlands). And we shared ideas as well, it wasn't like 'this is my idea and I'm not sharing it with anybody, you do what I'm doing'.
> Participant 2: Some children came with grandparents, so everybody was willing to help them as well.
> Participant 1: Some came from like big families, and there was maybe the one child out of that family that was coming, so it would have been difficult for Mum to come.

5.7   Enjoyment and fun

Of the 31 participants interviewed, 24 had enjoyed projects 'very much', six had enjoyed it 'some' and one had 'no feelings either way'. A total of 29 said they would 'like to do more projects like this', one was 'not sure' and one said 'no'.

> Out of the whole group of people I was the quietest one out of the lot of them. They were all up for a laugh but I just sat down... I got a hell of a lot louder and was able to have more fun that I used to be able to. As ___ said after we did the last play, I actually stand up straight now because I used to slouch a lot.
> Participant

> We've had fun, laughs along the way. I've not done anything like this before and it's been fun. I've been enjoying it.
> Participant

> It's good craic, to get away from yourself and have a real laugh.
> Participant

> I really enjoyed it. I liked meeting new people – it was fun.
> Participant

5.8   Project-specific outcomes

Participants also benefited from arts projects in very particular ways, often reflecting the particular aims of projects. For example, the drama projects and

Connections, which used literature as a tool for exploring human behaviour, encouraged participants to see things from others' point of view. This was particularly powerfully felt by participants doing *Connections* – there were examples of participants identifying with fictional characters, situations or emotions and these were revealed in the discussions and in participants' notes and final essays (see Appendix 1). Most of the men that completed the course felt there was a time where either a text, or something someone had said within one of the subsequent discussions, hit a raw nerve or was particularly enlightening.

> Other people are something [to think about], it's changed my outlook on quite a lot and how people perceive me. We did quite a lot of that on certain things about how people felt about certain actions. It makes me think a bit more now about how people feel about my actions and how I feel about their actions.
> Participant

> When a raw nerve was hit and I disclosed things from my past that really affected me they [the Therapeutic Community] would help me. I left, at least seven times out of ten, I left those sessions carrying a lot in my mind, just chewing over. I left with so much in my head relating to me that I'd sit back and go over it again and work out why a piece of text managed to develop into me, going to places that it did.
> Participant

> I'm not a great lover of chemical misuse but I sat there and I was listening to one guy who did use a lot of drugs at one time and he was defending one side of the story and another guy was shouting him down. And you listen to both sides… you could see it from both angles.
> Participant

Vita Nova, a theatre group for recovering addicts, was another project which had very project-specific objectives which included complementing members' ongoing recovery, improving members' self-esteem and challenging stereotypes of who an addict is (see Appendix 1). Interviews with a sample of Vita Nova members (and the facilitator/director's own research) suggest the theatre group has supported people's ongoing recovery by raising members' self-esteem and confidence, providing a structure and a supportive and safe environment and, through the company's education work, offering members a way of giving something back.

5.9   Summary

There was evidence to suggest that participation in the arts had the following effects for most of the people interviewed:

- raised levels of self-esteem and confidence – as a result of projects people said they felt proud of what they had achieved, felt more confident and many felt better about themselves
- enhanced a feeling of self-determination and sense of control – participants felt they had had freedom to develop their ideas and, although fewer participants felt they had had a say over what happened in sessions, they generally felt a strong sense of ownership of the final product
- pleasure and enjoyment
- developed arts and creative skills, appreciation of the art, positive attitudes to the arts and a taste for more

People made new acquaintances but also friends who they felt they would continue to be friends with once projects had ended. Some projects, such as the drama projects, had a stronger group focus than others but most participants felt they were part of a team and were proud of what the group had achieved.

It proved impossible to explore community impacts in any rigour because of the absence of community-led projects in the research. One of the projects, *Telling Tales*, focused on a particular community and certainly some of its participants felt the project had generated a sense of community belonging and community spirit.[24] Similarly, many of the participants in *Vita Nova*, an ongoing drama project for people in recovery, said that as a result of the project they felt a stronger sense of belonging to a community (both the recovery community but also the community of Boscombe). It would be very valuable if future research were to explore a sample of preferably long-term, community-orientated projects using social capital theories – this was something that this particular research inquiry could not explore.

Outcomes have been explored in a fairly generalised way because of the variety of projects included in the sample. Clearly research evaluating projects that are explicitly seeking to improve people's health, create employment opportunities, reduce rates of re-offending and so on, would be best placed to show whether

---

[24] Case study 9.

the arts do indeed have such effects. The question of what participants do when projects are over has also not been addressed in this study – longitudinal research would be needed to assess whether outcomes are long-lasting and the extent to which people's stated intentions are followed through.

6 Partnerships

6.1 What is a partnership?

Partnership is a word that is frequently used but which can mean many different things. In the case study projects there were examples of partners that worked largely independently of each other (to the extent of each partner delivering largely 'stand-alone' projects) and there were partners that worked more closely but where there was a strict demarcation of roles and responsibilities.[25] Some non-arts partners provided access to participants or assisted arts organisations to recruit participants, some contributed funding towards projects and some provided specific expertise in working with particular groups (eg youth workers). There were some case study projects where partnerships ran smoothly, but more often than not there were difficulties of one sort or another; as one artist put it, 'partnerships are not easy!'

6.2 Partnerships initiated by an external agency

The partnerships set up by external agencies raised a number of issues – the whole dynamic was quite different from that in other projects, particularly when external agencies had gone as far as to suggest what the project might look like and how it might be delivered. As one partner explained, 'it wasn't like we sat down and said we want to do this joint project together, this is our aim, these are our objectives and this is our end goal'. In this particular case the partners, on reflection, felt they needed to have a more active role in shaping the project from the start. Further, the external agency had taken the lead in developing the aims and objectives of the project – they were not embedded in people's or community's needs: 'I think it's that thing of knowing the groups you're working with and setting aims and objectives that are directly relevant to them'.

Some organisations had been partnered up to work on things together but on reflection wondered if another partner might have been more appropriate. Intervention appeared to work most successfully when an organisation had freedom to select a partner and work with that agency in developing a project proposal.

The model 3 projects were brokered by the Arts Council and the agencies involved learned many lessons, which was part of the reason for them setting

---

[25] Examples of joint working were rare.

them up. While the partnerships were not always easy, many of the problems they experienced were ones that were also encountered by other partnerships.

6.3   Partnership challenges

The most trouble-free partnerships seemed to develop relatively naturally. They tended to have very clear and straightforward aims and objectives, the project fitted the respective organisations' goals, each organisation was honest about the resources it could commit to the project and roles and responsibilities were discussed and agreed at the outset.

> It fitted very well with the way we were working... We can genuinely say we were building on work and existing partnerships and relationships.
> Project partner

> It was really refreshing to work on a project that had clear aims and objectives, that we knew what we were trying to do, we knew what the roles were – almost 100% clear about things from the start.
> Project partner

Some partnerships did not evolve so naturally and organisations traced some of the difficulties they experienced back to the planning process; there needed to be more time spent discussing and establishing a way of working together.

> Probably we didn't set the agenda to get what we wanted out of the project... we needed more time to plan the project and be clear what we wanted to get out of it.
> Project partner

> Looking back the project would have benefited from setting up an ethos, a method of work so that there was more clarity at the start about roles and responsibilities. If a number of different people have involvement in a project then the description of roles and responsibilities has to be more detailed so that everyone knows.
> Project partner

Some partnerships had communication difficulties; either things were not communicated at all or things were misunderstood or misinterpreted.

We haven't always communicated very well why we've done what we've done, why we've made the decisions we did. If we had realised this earlier on it would have saved heartache.
Project partner

On marketing, we didn't work together on it. We should have put our heads together, identified who does what well, and worked from there. We didn't know dates for marketing about events, we weren't invited into workshops. I think people didn't want to risk excessive communication, particularly because time was limited, but communication was at the crux of making it work for everyone.
Project partner

6.4   Appreciating difference

Different ways of working

Partnerships sometimes brought together organisations that had very different ways of working. There was one example where one partner liked to work in a very ordered way and the other preferred to work more organically, while in other projects, organisations shared common ground (eg visual arts) but were coming at it from completely different points of view (from a gallery perspective or a community arts perspective). Sometimes such differences, although acknowledged, were difficult to overcome.

Big organisation versus small organisation

When large and small organisations worked together, one of the issues that was sometimes problematic, was the time taken to make decisions. While one organisation, because it was small and had senior staff closely involved, could make decisions quickly, the larger organisation needed more time.

We are a small community arts organisation where a staff member tends to do everything. They have different officers with different responsibilities and different people will have involvement in any one project. It has been agreed by both of us that the lines of communication could have been clearer. There have been blips and confusion that didn't need to happen.
Project partner

67

6.5   Partnerships with non-arts agencies

Statutory and other agencies would be better placed to tackle some of the problems associated with social exclusion than arts organisations working in isolation. Some organisations had recognised this and, for example, involved youth services so projects could use the specialist skills of a youth worker. There were some examples of very successful, mutually beneficial partnerships that had evolved over time such as that between Mercury Theatre and the North Essex Youth Offending Team or Bournemouth Theatre in Education and Dorset Police (see Appendix 1). However, some of the partnerships arts organisations had with non-arts agencies were relatively passive and amounted to little more than an agency 'hosting' a project. In the research, there were examples of projects where passive partners had had a negative impact on outcomes and committed partners had had the opposite effect.

> [What artists wanted] Someone to help with publicity, to put up posters and things... to go round and talk to participants and say are you interested, tell them about the course and... see how things are developing. In one centre we were left on our own, they wouldn't even ask how the outreach session had gone, they weren't really bothered.
> Artist

> It's been frustrating and demoralising. There have been times when we have had things set up and maybe we've been promised youth work support or volunteer support and that's not turned up... they've not delivered their side of the bargain, a particular session hasn't been set up or the centre's not been open.
> Project partner

> Particularly when you go to people and say we've got money to work with your group, when we first started doing that, it threw up problems because people say 'oh yeah, I'll do it'. Where you're a youth worker or someone working with people with disabilities, of course when it's so difficult to get money for people to work with you, they'll all say 'yes, yes, yes'.
> Artist

Partnerships often worked best where there were enthusiastic and supportive staff or volunteers working in partner agencies – that person could be a head teacher in a school, a volunteer working in a community centre or the coordinator of a community group.

> We knew it would be a good partnership or expected it to be because we knew the organisation and that they wouldn't use it as a chance to put their feet up, which is what happens with some groups. In order to avoid that we carefully chose, in fact we even interviewed respective groups.
> Artist

One difficulty was that partnerships often relied on an enthusiast – when they moved on, the arts organisation found itself in the position of having to rebuild relationships (if the contact was replaced) or, in the worst case scenario, was left with no contact at all and had to progress projects as best they could. This obviously had an impact on the sustainability of projects.

6.6   Summary

Partnership projects highlighted the importance of:

- setting clear aims and objectives that were understood by partners
- delivering projects that naturally fitted with organisations' respective goals
- being realistic about the level of contribution individual partners could make
- discussing how the partnership would work, particularly as organisations can be so different. For example, in the research there were partners who were coming from different places and had different organisational objectives (eg a venue perspective or a community arts perspective), had different ways of working (eg 'organic' or ordered), were very different sizes (eg large organisations had many departments and specialised functions while in small organisations one or two people did everything)
- creating strong partnerships with non-arts agencies

However, even if these principles are followed external factors can change and have a negative impact on partnerships. For example, the research highlighted the important role individuals play in making partnerships and projects work but if they move on mid-project this can have a significant impact on a project's progress.

7 Sustainability

A number of the case study projects had hoped to achieve some level of sustainability or had long-term goals. This chapter explores the approaches organisations used to achieve this and some of the reasons why achieving sustainability proved difficult. It considers sustainability in terms of offering participants pathways for continuity, as well as the sustainability of organisations or this type of arts activity.

7.1 Why sustain activity?

The Oxford Dictionary definition of sustain is 'to maintain or keep going continuously'. In the arts 'sustainability' has become something of a buzz word but it would clearly not be practical for arts organisations themselves to keep projects going indefinitely – there are finite resources and organisations need to consider their own development (as well as that of the groups they work with). Further, it is not always appropriate for projects to continue. For example, the facilitators of *Connections*, a 10-week course where prisoners used excerpts from literature to explore their behaviour, felt the course's brief and intense nature was one of the course's strengths. In other instances, participants quite simply did not want to continue beyond the term of the project. That projects end, was not necessarily viewed as an argument for them not happening:

> I think too often, in too many cases, issues around sustainability are used to prevent the work being done in the first place and I think that's wrong. Agreed, doing the work creates expectations or opens windows that people didn't know existed and they want to do more. Where do they go – that seems a different matter. We are attempting to create the conditions that there is something to go for, something else. It would be like they taste a particular food that was fantastic and they can't buy it – it doesn't invalidate the experience.
> Director/facilitator

However, artists and project coordinators felt there was a moral duty not to 'parachute in' to communities, deliver a project and then run. Practitioners wanted, where possible, to offer those participants avenues for continuing or progressing, if that is what they wanted.

7.2 Exit strategies

Where there was no plan to continue activity or progression, organisations used several methods to end projects sensitively. First and foremost it was felt important not to raise the expectation that an activity would continue and not to make promises that could not be kept. Organisations also sought to end projects in a positive way, through a trip to see an exhibition of their work or a certificate presentation, for example. One organisation was aware that following the highs of performance, participants experienced a low and so had built in a post-project debrief where participants came together to talk about their experience.

In situations where participants were interested in continuing or progressing their involvement in arts, yet arts organisations had no plans to continue delivering an activity, practitioners said they would try to signpost people on to other groups or classes if they could. One organisation was purposely working to integrate its work into the larger programme of community arts projects taking place in the area and planned on informing past participants of opportunities being delivered by other organisations. However, 'signposting' was often viewed as an unsatisfactory approach and for various reasons: sometimes there was very little to 'signpost' people on to, existing arts groups had long waiting lists, participants had been banned from mainstream activities such as youth clubs, participants who showed some interest in entering education did not easily 'fit' into the formal education system, and so on.

> It would be good to direct people to other resources but there's very little available in this area.
> Artist

> The difficulty in terms of exit strategies is that some of these youngsters they still require a level of support that other students might not need... they still need the taxi if you like. That's what's missing.
> Director/facilitator

Even when artists and project partners and coordinators had attempted to end projects sensitively they sometimes felt uncomfortable about giving people something and then taking it away.

It's like they've come in from the cold and they're turned out again. Some will just say that was good and get on with things, but for some the intensity of it opens up a new avenue and that is then taken away.
Project partner

You do feel bad just leaving it – particularly for the residents, you've built up relations with them and you feel you're letting them down really.
Artist

It was one of the first things I asked about when the project came up because it looks like a reasonably big investment and if it was just going to be an exercise and then bye, well you can feel like an absolute shit 'bye and hope it goes alright'. You know that everything will just close up behind you and then that will be that.
Artist

It you go back to a group and say 'oh we did that lovely project with you before, it was a real shame it ended'. And it's sort of bitter-sweet for them, because they were involved in something good and it ended.
Project partner

7.3   Approaches used to sustain activity

Capacity-building

For staff and volunteers in participant groups
Three case study organisations in the research aimed to inspire staff, volunteers or participants in the groups they worked with to lead activities themselves once the artists had left. However, this approach was not without problems: some volunteers or staff built up some level of creative skills but then left their respective organisations; there was not always anyone with an interest in taking up the role; people did not necessarily feel confident about leading activity at the time projects ended; some staff felt that the ideal arts model was to have professional artists deliver and lead activities rather than to do it themselves.

For artists
Several projects attempted to address the shortage of artists with the skills and experience needed to work in social inclusion contexts by building in an element of training provision. For example, the Unit for the Arts and Offenders piloted two training courses for professional artists, Mantle Arts recruited a less experienced

artist to work alongside a team of experienced artists, while *Telling Tales* provided artists with training so they could deliver arts activities for children under 5.

Building programmes of planned activity

One organisation, reflecting on its own development, noted that for many years it had lurched from project to project but now focused on creating 'programmes' of work as far as that was possible. This gave them some freedom to return to groups but also allowed them to work with new groups.

> What we are conscious of is doing a project for ten weeks and then leaving. It's one of the downfalls; we go in, it's great but what then? It's a continuous problem. How do we avoid that? One way is to set up a programme of work rather than running individual projects… It's one of those things we strive to do. As the development side of our work with groups, we always like to offer and encourage a group that we've worked with to want to do more work…. So it's part of that thing of once you've worked with a group and they've enjoyed it and moved forward we like to offer them a chance to move further forward.
> Artist

Creating pathways for progression

Some organisations had experimented with establishing progression routes:

- the Mercury Theatre established a theatre group which graduates of its summer residencies for young offenders could join
- what was originally going to be a one-off drugs education project at Bournemouth Theatre in Education evolved into a regular theatre group and eventually an independent theatre company
- the writer in residence at HMP Channings Wood ran an intensive course for graduates in response to requests from *Connections* participants for more
- Jubilee Arts was developing a 'drop-in' resource

Other organisations maintained contact with participants by inviting participants to occasional large-scale 'open access' community events, such as lantern parades.

7.4   Barriers

The research identified a variety of reasons why achieving sustainability can be difficult.

Sustainability is not addressed in a timely way

There were some instances where organisations had, at the start of projects, agreed that finding a way of sustaining activity was important but then either it failed to be followed through or the issue was left too late to address. For example:

- one project established lots of partnerships and raised expectation. Although the issue of how to fund future activity was discussed this was not followed through and applications were only made as the project was drawing to its conclusion
- in another project, partners noted it was important to address the issue and, over the course of the project, made contact with some non-arts agencies and considered various options but sustainability was not secured at the time the project ended
- one very small-scale organisation had plans to apply for funds to maintain some level of activity but the person with that responsibility left the organisation and, because it was a small organisation, there were no staff to take on that task

Further, there was at least one project that had long-term aims and required partners to be responsible for continuing activity themselves once the project ended. However, in practice partners played a quite passive role in the project – if they were to be responsible for continuing the project a far greater degree of investment in the long-term goals of the project would be needed.

Funding

Short-term
Opportunities for long-term planning were hampered by the short-term nature of much funding. Organisations may have aspirations to work on a more continuous basis in geographic areas or with particular groups but the reality for many was that activity could only be planned and delivered in a relatively haphazard way.

> Funding is an issue, it's not difficult to get project funding but it's more difficult to say 'can we have additional money just in case someone wants to do some additional work?' As they would say, quite rightly I suppose, 'do it properly through accredited training' and so on but that's not us.
> Artist

Some arts practitioners noted that that one of the difficulties with a lot of funding was that funders liked supporting things that were new but, as one artist put it, 'sustainability is not quite as sexy'.

Level of investment
Some of the activity taking place in this field requires a relatively large-scale investment because it involves working with small numbers of participants and requires a high artist-participant ratio. However, as a member of a youth offending team noted , 'I guess in terms of how much does it cost per child it's very expensive but the reality is locking a youngster up and that's expensive too'.

One of the model 3 organisations noted that the way the project had been funded had enabled them to work in a particular way with a particular group of people. However, in reality that work was not sustainable – they would find it difficult to maintain that level of investment.

Dependence on individuals and small agencies

Many projects were initiated by individuals and delivered by freelance artists or small arts organisations – they are the catalysts for ideas and drive the work forward. However, many had demanding workloads and at points seemed stretched to meet the demands being placed on them.

> … for an organisation like us now there's never been such a good time for diversity for funding, that's partly because of the lottery and trusts and stuff like that are really more attuned to this area of work. But there's no way we can do all the work, even just the work that's available here… We're having to turn down work which is nice (for us) but for the field of work it's how are we going to get through this?
> Artist

Lack of artists with necessary skills

Some organisations felt it was difficult to find artists with the relevant skills and experience to deliver work of high quality. It was a problem that one artist traced back to artists' training which she argued offered a very narrow definition of arts practice, 'you sit there and wait for Saatchi to come along or whoever and you engage with critical debate about arts practice and all that kind of stuff. There is still this feeling that the aim is to get your work into galleries'.

Weak partnerships

There was a view that creating partnerships with non-arts agencies was one way of securing sustainability since some arts activity was contributing to other organisations' objectives. However, partnerships with non-arts agencies were often relatively passive, so when the arts project ended there was no commitment on their part to secure future investment or continue activity.

7.5   Summary

The research suggests that there may be a number of reasons why achieving sustainability is difficult:

- funding issues – funding tends to be short-term, the levels of investment required are sometimes high and funders are interested in supporting new and innovative projects rather than enabling activity to continue
- weak partnerships – non-arts agencies may be happy to 'host' an activity or play a relatively passive role but are not always the committed partners arts organisations might hope for
- dependence on individuals and small organisations/skills shortage – some interviewees felt there was a shortage of artists with the necessary skills to work in this area
- organisations sometimes did not tackle the sustainability issue seriously enough, early enough. For example, organisations approached potential partners or applied for funding when projects were drawing to a conclusion

Partnerships with non-arts agencies were sometimes identified as one way of safeguarding the sustainability of activity but partnerships in themselves do not guarantee a project's future – the partnerships have to be strong and involve agencies with a long-term perspective.

8   Evaluation and success

This chapter looks at different evaluation approaches and complements the work conducted by Moriarty (2002) in the self-evaluation strand of the research programme.

8.1   Approaches to evaluation

There are different philosophical positions that influence the evaluation approach people adopt and different understandings of what evaluation is (see Jermyn, 2001). However, *Sharing Practice*, the publication resulting from the self-evaluation strand of the social exclusion research programme, differentiates between monitoring, advocacy, documentation and evaluation:

> Evaluation and monitoring are not the same. Monitoring involves regular measurement of progress against declared objectives. It accounts for the use of resources – public, community and personal. It provides evidence of effective and efficient delivery and is likely to be a basic requirement for receiving public funding (Moriarty, 2002).

Artists and project coordinators when asked how, if at all, they would be evaluating projects, sometimes described how they intended to monitor the numbers and types of participants engaging in activity. Their evaluation approach involved primarily collecting monitoring data and perhaps supplementing this with some documentary evidence such as photographs or a video.

Many described a model of evaluation which involved setting aims and objectives and assessing whether these had been met (what Moriarty, 2002, refers to as monitoring) Those organisations that did not set aims and objectives could not, of course, use this model.

> We have a set procedure which we follow each time. We've got our aims, we have our objectives. And then, depending on the nature of the group or the artist we're working with, we ask them for feedback. So it could be written, it could be verbal, we have photographic evidence as well but usually we ask for comments. And those comments are related back to our original aims and objectives.
> Project coordinator

I think we're good at doing this for projects. We've adapted the Woolf guidelines to funders' requirements – setting aims and objectives and measurable outcomes are the basis of all projects.[26]
Project partner

Others described a model which involved assessing whether aims and objectives had been met but also looking more generally at what worked and what did not eg looking at the project in much broader terms than its aims and objectives.

We have a model of self-evaluation that underpins all our work. Basically, this can be summed up as what is working/worked? What is not working/didn't work? What can be done better/to rectify – and how? Evaluation tools are built into projects from the outset, particularly by identifying concrete and measurable aims and objectives, and by establishing anticipated outcomes… Because I'm thinking what can we organise better or how can we do things better structurally and those sorts of things. We're talking about how do we feed what we've learned through that process back into the work that we do? Are we artists who worked on that programme better actors or better artists, or if not, better informed?
Artist

It [evaluation] is fundamentally different from monitoring, monitoring is really just us looking at what it is we did, what we said we'd do and assessing any differences between those two things. It doesn't really address the value or the nature of those differences particularly because they're kind of determined aren't they? If you're hoping to get 30 people into a session and only 25 come – then that's the assessment of it… I just think the evaluation tells some much more valuable stories than that… We are interested in what the intentions of the project are but also what the frustrations of the projects are, the things which for one reason or another are frustrating or prevent things being achievable.
Tutor

Some organisations evaluated everything while others were more selective, as one artist said, 'you have to pick and choose what you evaluate and do an evaluation that's appropriate to the project'.

---

[26] The guidelines referred to are those found in *Partnership for learning* (Woolf, 1999) . This was a guide to evaluating arts education projects published by the former Arts Council of England and Regional Arts Boards.

A number of organisations built evaluation into projects at the outset and had a set procedure for deciding the shape and direction the evaluation would take. For example, one middle-scale, established organisation always set three objectives for a project and then made decisions about what formal evaluation needed to take place in relation to each objective, standard monitoring and evaluation forms were always completed and there was a company debrief in which things learned were fed back into organisation. Other organisations, particularly small and emerging organisations, had no set monitoring or evaluation procedures and had a more ad hoc approach to evaluation.

8.2 Methods of evaluation

The practitioners interviewed in the course of this research used a variety of different methods and these are discussed briefly below (see also Moriarty, 2002).

Participant feedback

Forms were one of the most common methods used to get feedback from participants. Organisations found these were easy to administer (although some people needed help to complete them) and useful for generating statistics and getting a certain level of feedback. However, these methods had some drawbacks – participants found forms off-putting and artists and project coordinators felt the depth of data was sometimes quite thin.

> They [the project assessors] wanted them to fill out forms at the end of every single workshop to say what they [the participants] had done. It just isn't possible – it's such a short space of time once you've set up everything and you've got to clear away at the end – it's just not feasible really… I think that would put people off – if they thought every single time they come they had to sit down and write something. And also, some of them can't write.
> Artist

> It was a series of questions with four or five options – good, middling, okay, you know. They were questions about the organisation of the project, about how the rehearsals went and then people could put more comments. And they were filled with over-the-top praise and delight, which was great, but I did feel they were a bit skinny, on-the-surface responses.
> Project coordinator

Well, generally one of our aims is to get people to achieve something they wouldn't have thought they could achieve. So obviously they're always going to say that was great, that was wonderful. One of the difficult things about evaluating through the group you're working with, is that unless you've really messed it up people say 'it was great'. We don't use the evaluation sheets very often now because generally people say, 'we loved it, I'm really proud of what I've done'. Which is good because that's what we're after but they're not likely to be critical when you've taken them on a journey they didn't expect to go on... Generally, the people we would ask that kind of question of would be the agencies we're in partnership with, so in a school [for example] it would be the teacher involved in the project.
Artist

Organisations had used other methods of getting feedback from participants such as video booths, videoing conversations as work was taking place and one-to-one interviews. One interviewee described how participants in one project had created pottery faces showing happy/unhappy expressions and at the end of the session they raised the face that showed how they felt. It was a variation on the smiley face/not smiley face responses offered in feedback forms which was initially fun (although the novelty of this approach wore off!).

That is a problem, about how you create sufficiently varied evaluation processes to capture the different means whereby people would like to make their comments. That's something that I would have liked to have done more of this year but haven't, but will do in the next two. What I want to do is make sure that people will have some ongoing means of evaluation, so through a kind of video commentary box or through tape diaries – that would be much more useful.
Project coordinator

One of the methods that worked very successfully, in the context of a drama project for young people, was having a debrief day where both artists and participants played some games and reflected back on the process as a group and in smaller subgroups (notes were kept of those discussions).

Participants in *Connections*, a course for prisoners, completed 'how I see myself' forms at the start and at the end of the project and also wrote an essay about their experience on the course (see Appendix 1). However, participants were aware that the final essays would be read by someone in Probation and this had an impact on how much information people were willing to divulge. Another organisation had used self-esteem tests as part of an attempt to get beyond an anecdotal approach and supply funders with 'hard' evidence.

Open House provided gatekeepers in community groups with training in evaluation methods. Each gatekeeper was responsible for coordinating venue visits, collecting feedback from group members and producing an evaluation report at the end of the project. This approach worked up to a certain level but, with further development, might have been more successful still.

Often artists referred to the informal discussions they had with participants as projects were taking place. However, this more 'informal' feedback was rarely noted down and used in evaluation reports – organisations seemed unsure about how best to make use of such data. Even when participant feedback had been collected using formal methods it was not always 'used' in reports.

Artist feedback

Many organisations had developed feedback forms for artists. The questions asked varied from organisation to organisation but often required artists to reflect on the things that worked well and the things that could be improved. Sometimes the same issues were addressed but informally through discussion at the end of workshops, sessions or rehearsals.

> The bit that has worked well is the fact that we have filled out evaluation forms at the end of each session – they were really valuable in looking back. We wrote down all the names and what happened in the lesson. So looking through those you get an impression of progression related to each participant or progression in the way the project has gone. So that's been good.
> Artist

Some organisations described how they had encountered difficulties getting feedback from freelance artists (the artists had not completed the forms that kept the organisation informed about what was happening in sessions). This was sometimes due to organisations not creating a successful structure in which organisations and freelance artists could work together from the outset (see Chapter 4).

Reflective records

Keeping a reflective record was felt to be valuable by those who did it but it was felt by some to be too time-consuming.

> I think the idea of keeping a journal and saying what you've done, what's been good, what you've had to change, can be useful and there has been a usefulness to it but it's so time-consuming. You do your evaluation and then you want to say: one hour evaluating time.
> Project partner

Stakeholder feedback

Stakeholder views were gathered through feedback forms, debrief meetings and interviews. This appeared to be a relatively trouble-free exercise, although one organisation working with passive partners had had difficulties getting them to complete and return forms.

External evaluator or objective insider

There are strengths and drawbacks to using external consultants or agencies to evaluate projects and these are articulated in Moriarty (2002). One arts organisation in the research had developed a long-term relationship with an evaluator and found this worked very successfully for them.

> ... ____ actually draws on our critical reflections, the spontaneous stuff all the time, so that's kind of enhancing and developing the quality of the procedure... I think it's really useful to have someone who has a lot of skill and knowledge about the process of evaluation and can bring that to bear, who will be consultative and will share that experience....
> Tutor

A number of arts organisations had, on occasion, used members of staff who were not delivering arts activity to sit in on sessions and record their observations; it was a method which appeared to work well.

Creative evaluation

Within the case studies there was little use made of creative evaluation and there was a certain amount of confusion as to what creative evaluation actually was. Creative evaluation methods are more closely aligned to the creative processes which might be used during arts projects. Examples provided by Moriarty (2002) include: time-line; image theatre; moving answers; bull's eye and big paper thinking. For example, one of the organisations participating in the research had hoped that participants would use photography to capture images of how they saw themselves before the project compared with after but in practice this proved difficult to carry out. One of the issues was how should artists interpret these creative outputs – there was a danger of imposing the wrong interpretation if its meaning was not clear.

> I haven't come across anyone yet who's doing creative evaluation. We talked about it didn't we right at the beginning? We talked about how we wanted to try and evaluate this [the project] creatively, has anybody got any ideas… and it never came to fruition and we didn't get any ideas. In the end I said 'well look, let's not force this because if nobody's got any ideas that we can try out, that we can pilot, then let's not go for it for the sake of it'. So we haven't done it.
> Project coordinator

8.3   What is success?

Artists were asked to consider the outcomes of the project, including any participant outcomes (see Chapter 2 and Appendix 2). However, artists were also asked how they judged the success of a project; often they referred to the seemingly small, yet significant, things they had witnessed which they felt were evidence of a successful outcome. For example, a participant printed out his name without any help; a person borrowed a book from the library because he had enjoyed reading an excerpt from it during a project; participants arrived early for sessions or asked for sessions to be longer. They would also reflect whether the group had met its potential and on the progression of the group and individuals.

> Some of it is just a feeling you get over the length of a project. So, for example, the ___ group…but they never realised their potential within that project. Their work has some good things in it but there could have been so much more…. for various reasons, we weren't getting the full potential

out of that group. We tried different ways of trying to make sure we did it but we didn't. Whereas, with the ___ group, they went past what we expected, their potential. That was obvious half way through the project, that they were going to achieve things we hadn't thought they could do.
Artist

I think all I would say is that I got a lot from it and I know other people got a lot from it in terms of their enjoyment, their achievement and their confidence… The process itself and the growth in people's confidence and skills…
Artist

Success is ___ bringing in his books, talking to his friends and family about the exhibition, for him to pick a phrase from his testimony. Another example, ___ originally when we mentioned writing, he said 'I don't want to do that'. We played a word association game and with the words from that he came up with a poem and he said 'I like that and I wrote it'.
Artist

Some referred to the direct feedback they gathered from participants and from group leaders.

The feedback we get from them – that's how we have to judge it. What feedback they give us. They don't pull punches or whatever the phrase is, they let you know if they don't think it's good. And the enthusiasm that they show and support for each other.
Facilitator

The judgements made by others, be they audiences, attenders or other groups, also informed artists' perceptions of whether a project had been a success or not.

I think a lot of it is what other people say about it. ___ has been doing a lot of getting links to other sites, so getting people to look at other sites and, as a matter of course, in doing that they look at the site and say that's really good, we'll use that.
Artist

I suppose unless everybody was lying – we've had so many people telling us it was good work. You're instinctively working towards things, giving notes, keeping it fresh… The audience loved it. I had someone in her final

year doing theatre studies who thought it was the real Shakespeare, it was authentic... She was an authority on Shakespeare and she loved it... We're doing it again due to popular demand.
Director/facilitator

8.4   Summary

The evaluation process ran smoothest when it was considered during the planning process and built into the project. The less successful evaluations were devised in a more ad hoc way and were more half-hearted in their approach. Small and emerging organisations sometimes struggled with evaluation – it was something they felt they should be doing but they did not have any set procedures or feel they had the skills and were often juggling a heavy workload so their time was limited.

A variety of different evaluation approaches were used. Methods that worked particularly well were often incorporated into the process. For example, artists had paid time at the end of sessions where they reflected on the project and recorded their observations. Organisations appeared to have most difficulty getting quality feedback from participants. However, the material that was collected from participants (through feedback forms or informal discussion for example) often did not appear in evaluation reports.

9   Conclusion

The former Arts Council of England and Regional Arts Boards identified three different models of social inclusion work occurring in the arts:

* model 1 was community-led work, where the initiative for the arts project came from a local community or group
* model 2 covered experienced arts organisations or companies supported through the Arts Council and Regional Arts Boards, for whom working with people from low income communities was a mainstay of their work
* model 3 covered partnerships brokered by the Arts Council between established, funded organisations with little or no experience of working with people and communities in low income areas and organisations with a track record of work in this field

However, the projects explored in the research did not neatly fit this typology. Apart from the model 3 partnerships, almost all projects fell into the model 2 category in that these were experienced arts organisations, companies, or artists supported by the Arts Council and Regional Arts Boards. Projects tended not to be initiated by local communities or groups but by artists or arts administrators working for arts organisations or Regional Arts Boards.[27] However, those projects were sometimes initiated in response to a perceived need, built on previous work or involved local communities or groups in shaping the project (although often only after project funding was secured). It is likely that in terms of the nature of community involvement there is a continuum of practice; it would be valuable to explore practice that appears on the 'community-led' end of the continuum in future research.

The projects were initiated in different ways, had different aims and objectives and involved different partnerships. The artists delivering projects had different ways of working and a wide range of arts and crafts were represented including digital arts, textiles, painting, mural making, photography, writing, music making and drama. Participating groups ranged from older people living in sheltered accommodation to families with children aged under 5 and projects took place in settings ranging from prisons to theatres, from community centres to hostels for the homeless. A rich body of data about practice has emerged due to the diversity of organisations and projects in the sample and this can be used to inform policy and advocacy initiatives.

---

[27] The regional New Audiences Programme projects were initiated by Regional Arts Boards who solicited applications from arts organisations and companies.

Although a wide range of practice was documented, the research prompts the question 'does it all count as social inclusion work?' The indicators of exclusion that were commonly referred to in government policy when the project was commissioned were health, education, employment and crime. The projects in this research worked with people living in poor neighbourhoods and with groups that some may define as excluded (although there is of course a definitional issue about which groups fit into this category) but they tended not to have aims that involved 'tackling' explicitly the four policy indicators.[28] Even those projects that involved working with offenders did not explicitly aim to reduce offending or recidivism (although the Youth Offending Team and prison in question felt these projects were supporting their organisational aims). Organisations' own evaluations did not use policy indicators as criteria for judging whether projects were successful or not – not surprising given these were not the explicit aims of projects. It is likely that even if projects had had these aims, evaluating whether these had been achieved in a rigorous way would be beyond the skills or abilities of arts practitioners. For example, to evaluate the impact of *Vita Nova's* drug education programme in a rigorous way would involve substantial resources.

There were participants interviewed in the course of this research who had stopped offending, who had taken up educational opportunities, who achieved qualifications or who had moved into employment and others who said they intended to pursue such options. Projects were not necessarily *the* sole causal factor – sometimes it appeared to play more of a contributory or catalytic role in changing people's lives. For example, Mercury Theatre's summer residency for young people worked best for those who were 'looking for an out', *Fast Forward* worked most successfully for those homeless people who were living relatively stable lives and *Vita Nova* supports the ongoing recovery of people who are already in treatment or have left treatment. Longitudinal research which involves long-term monitoring of participants would be necessary to evaluate the extent to which the arts have long-lasting effects.

Some arts practitioners argued that exclusion from leisure and cultural opportunities is one dimension of social exclusion; from this perspective social exclusion is being addressed by increased participation in arts and cultural

---

[28] That is not to say these projects do not take place at all but a research project that hoped to explore these outcomes more specifically would have required different criteria for selecting organisations and projects.

activities by excluded individuals or groups. Of course, turning this argument around, one can also say that the arts can be excluding.

Several projects had aims that referred to outcomes such as confidence, esteem or skills. Interviews with participants showed that they felt more confident as a result of projects, that they felt proud of what they and their group had achieved and that they had learned new skills and developed existing skills through the arts process (some of which were transferable to work or educational settings). Longitudinal research would be required to establish the extent to which such outcomes are long-lasting, transfer to other settings or pave the way to other things.

There is, of course, an argument for saying there is value in participating in arts activities purely for the experience itself; art for art's sake. Participants felt projects were a source of fun and enjoyment, that they had broadened their horizons and, in some cases, had improved their quality of life. Participants had had the opportunity to be creative and use their imaginations; the arts outputs ranged from 'Scratter the Sea Monster' that headed the Coalville Lantern Parade to a silver key ring one school-aged participant designed and produced for her grandfather.

The Arts Council needs to communicate clearly what it views as social inclusion work and how this is different from access or audience development. The Arts Council's definition in *Addressing social exclusion: a framework for action* 'takes low-income areas as its starting point and focuses particularly on poverty in combination with other factors such as low educational attainment, poor health, crime and unemployment' and notes that 'expanding access has always been an important part of the work of the funding system… Advocating the role the arts can play in addressing social exclusion is however a new departure...' (ACE, 1999). This definition needs further unpicking and clarification.

One of the aims of the research was to identify characteristics of successful initiatives. Success factors and lessons learned are explored in more detail in the stand-alone case studies (see Appendix 1). In many ways the good practice principles identified through the research will not be 'news' to arts practitioners or policy makers but they need to be restated nevertheless:

- clear aims and objectives that are worked through in terms of project delivery eg projects with long-term goals need to build in mechanisms for achieving those

- enough lead-in time and planning: research and recruitment of participants, development of partnerships, recruiting artists, finding appropriate venues and so on are all tasks that are a necessary part of the research and planning of projects
- strong partnerships: the model 3 and other partnerships highlighted the importance of agreeing and understanding aims and objectives; of projects 'fitting' with organisations' respective goals; of establishing an effective way of working together which involves being clear about roles and responsibilities; of good communication
- sustainability and exit strategies: the future welfare of participants needs to be considered at the outset of projects – this might explore building partnerships with organisations that are willing to make a long-term investment in arts initiatives or at the very least thinking about how to bring projects to a closure
- artists' approach: flexible working methods, 'democratic' structures, quality and the importance of providing one-to-one were recurrent themes

Successful partnerships with non-arts agencies were often reliant on an individual or volunteer who supported the arts initiative; this obviously means some 'partnerships' were relatively fragile, which had implications for the future sustainability or continuity of activity.

In considering sustainability there is the sustainability of participants' involvement in the arts as well as the continuation and development of the sector itself. Several organisations noted that there was a shortage of appropriately skilled artists and organisations themselves were sometimes struggling to manage workloads. Other barriers that made achieving sustainability difficult included the short-term nature of much funding. Organisations that want to work in a more strategic way can be hampered from doing so because they were essentially project funded. The weak nature of partnerships also was a barrier to securing sustainability. There may be value in the Arts Council exploring successful, long-term partnerships in depth and disseminating the lessons learned.

Organisations had used a range of methods to evaluate projects; there were examples of projects that had been evaluated comprehensively and others where evaluation was more superficial. Some 'evaluations' primarily entailed collecting monitoring data and documenting projects (eg photographs, video etc) while others were more detailed and built in some means for collecting feedback from participants or stakeholders. Formal evaluation, in terms of collecting and assimilating data, generally ended soon after project activity ended (even when projects had long-term aims). Collected data was not always 'used.' There were, for example, cases where participants or stakeholders completed forms but the data was not referred to in evaluation reports. Some organisations used a model of evaluation which involved setting aims and objectives and at the end reflecting back on the extent to which those aims and objectives were met. However, the value of the evaluation in such circumstances does to a great extent depend on the nature of the aims and objectives set and the measures people use to assess whether they have been met or not.

One potential success indicator might have been the extent to which organisations met their aims and objectives. A scan through the 15 case studies will reveal how much variation there is in the nature of objectives set by the organisations: some set objectives which could be reached relatively easily while others set more challenging goals; some had objectives that focused on reaching certain numbers of people, some on achieving an end product (eg to create a play) and some on achieving outcomes (eg to raise confidence); some focused on the short term and others on the long term (eg to inspire an arts group to continue). It is difficult to judge the success or failure of projects purely on whether they meet their stated aims and objectives because you are not comparing like with like. Further, aims and objectives were sometimes not met but other unpredicted outcomes were achieved, as well as important learning.

The research explored using indicators which quantified qualitative outcomes such as whether participants felt better about themselves, felt proud of what they had achieved and so on. However, as some arts practitioners pointed out unless organisations are doing a terrible job, participants will provide positive responses. Further, indicators can be ambiguous and considerable care is needed in interpreting their meaning. A project is not a failure because a participant did not feel better about themselves at the end of the process (they might simply have felt fantastic at the start!) and if someone does not want to do a similar project again that does not mean it was a bad experience (for example, one *Connections* participant would not want to do a similar project because he had found it a draining, but nonetheless beneficial and enjoyable, experience). Further, to find indicators that can be used across projects in a sector where practice is *so* diverse and tell us something meaningful will be a very problematic task – particularly any indicators that rely on collecting data from participants since project attendance can be erratic, not all participants will complete projects and some projects are 'drop-in' by nature. What may be possible is to build up a pool of indicators for use in groups of projects that have explicit aims in terms of impacting on health, education, employment or crime or indicators that focus on practice.

Appendix 1: Case studies

A.1.1: Connections

Summary

Organisation: HMP Channings Wood, Devon
Activity: a reading group used literature to explore aspects of human nature and offending behaviour
Facilitators: team of five prison staff including Mary Stephenson, writer in residence, and Neil Galbraith, education tutor
Budget: a Regional Arts Lottery Programme award of £66,000 financed a programme of activities including *Connections*
Dates: each *Connections* course comprised ten 1½ hour discussion sessions - this case study focuses on the course that ran from 24 April to 26 June 2002
Participants: offenders
Arts Council research: interviews with the writer in residence, course leader, Governor of Inmate Activities, eight participants at the start of the course and six participants who completed the course at the end (nine in total); observation
Outputs

- seven of the 12 participants who enrolled on the course completed it
- participants read texts by a range of different writers, including Shakespeare, Charles Dickens, Ken Kesey, John Steinbeck and Irvine Welsh
- participants discussed a range of different themes including greed and ambition, guilt, manipulation, violence, control, relationships and dreams

The philosophy underlying *Connections* was that we can use stories to understand ourselves; it gives us space to make the connection between somebody in a story and ourselves.

Twelve participants enrolled on the *Connections* course running from 24 April to 26 June 2002. Participants came to sessions having read a pre-selected text and then discussed the piece and how it related to them. Discussions took place in a democratic forum, where prisoners' views were as valid as everybody else's round the table and where there were no right or wrong answers.

The texts were selected so as to prompt discussion about particular aspects of human nature that might have relevance to offending behaviour. For example, Shakespeare's *Macbeth* was used to discuss ambition, greed and guilt and *Oliver Twist* by Charles Dickens was used to discuss manipulation. Other texts included *Of Mice and Men* (John Steinbeck), *Sea Wolf* (Jack London) and *One Flew Over the Cuckoo's Nest* (Ken Kesey).

After each session, participants wrote up notes on what they thought about the text and the discussion, and at the end of the course they wrote essays on what they had learned (copies of which were shared with the group and were sent to Probation).

Writer in residence at HMP Channings Wood

HMP Channings Wood is a modern purpose-built category C training prison which contains a Therapeutic Unit for tackling drug abuse and a Vulnerable Prisoner Unit which specialises in sex offender treatment programmes.

Mary Stephenson was appointed as writer in residence at the prison in 1998. Her post was initially funded through an Arts Council residency scheme and involved her supporting and developing prisoners' creative writing on a one-to-one basis and the production of the monthly prison magazine. Over the years, funding from other sources was secured, notably a Regional Arts Lottery Programme (RALP) award which was used to set up and run: a prison radio station (*Con Air*); a programme in which prisoners wrote and illustrated basic adult education books relevant to a prison audience (*Con Texts*); and a reading group that explored offending behaviour through literature (*Connections*).

Aims and objectives

To begin with, Stephenson did not write out any aims and objectives because she wanted to be flexible and see what could be achieved. However, she felt there were always subconscious aims and objectives and these came to be formalised as:

- to read and discuss the stories and characters in the light of our experiences and reactions to them
- to see whether we can better understand ourselves and each other through the stories/characters
- to explore parts of ourselves we might not have thought about in our recent past
- to think of ourselves in terms of self-esteem, confidence, empathy with others – not in terms of actual offences committed, but in terms of how we saw ourselves, how we see ourselves now and how we would like to see ourselves

The RALP funded activity as a whole also had aims around benefiting a certain number of prisoners.

The facilitators did not view *Connections* as a course that 'addressed' offending behaviour; rather it explored related behaviour such as self-esteem, confidence, control, empathy and relationships.

> There is a personal identification there but it has to reach them not just at the level of recognition, but also at the level of 'I was like that'. That then

becomes confessional, 'this is how I was like Sykes, this is how I was like Othello, I can understand, I can see what happens there'. And I think on the whole that's about as far as we can get… In other words, we never get to the point where we're confronting and actively challenging causations in terms of offending behaviour. What we're looking at is can you empathise with the text, can you relate to it in terms of your own relationships, can you think about this in terms of incidences in your own life?
Course leader

Project planning and management

Connections was inspired by *Changing Lives Through Literature*, a programme developed by Professor Robert Waxler at the University of Massachusetts and run successfully in Massachusetts and other states. Having heard about this model, Stephenson went about developing a programme that could be run in HMP Channings Wood.

Discussions were held with prison colleagues to ensure *Connections* linked in to what other departments were doing. However, Stephenson was keen that the course should have an arts-led focus and she steered away from the accreditation route which she felt would change the nature of the course. Approval from the Governors was also achieved to ensure that *Connections* was officially recognised by the prison.

In 2000, *Connections* was piloted with a group of prisoners who were asked to advise the staff team on the most effective way of delivering the course. This was a useful exercise – the participants made a number of suggestions which came to be built into future courses.

Recruitment of facilitators

There were generally five staff facilitators on each *Connections* course and they were expected to attend each of the 10-week sessions. The facilitators tried to create a relaxed environment which was in keeping with the democratic nature of the group where prisoners' views were as valid as everyone else's round the table.

Neil Galbraith, a member of the prison's education staff, was viewed as the obvious person to lead the course because of his English Literature background. His time on *Connections* was paid but all the other facilitators were volunteers.[29] Having someone on the team with a literature background was felt to be valuable although that is not to say that the whole team were literature experts; one of the

---

[29] When submitting the funding application Stephenson had believed that the time staff spent facilitating the course would be counted against their work, but this was not the case. If doing the project again she would budget for facilitators to be paid or to have time off in lieu.

facilitators was a self-confessed non-reader to begin with and another regarded himself as a slow reader.

An important part of Galbraith's role was to identify the key questions raised through the text and try to get as much discussion around those as possible. Over time he became more direct in his approach but he was always reluctant to corner groups and 'close down' space.

> I think the difficulty has always really been the sort of bridge, the discussion about the books to the discussion about them. I think I've got better at it, in the sense that I'm much simpler and more directive.
> Course leader

The staff team also included a prison officer and someone with counselling skills. Security is always a consideration in a prison and if a prison officer had not been on the team then supervision would have to be arranged. With prisoners' emotional support in mind, Stephenson also arranged for Listeners who had completed past *Connections* courses to be available to speak to participants.[30]

> It is something that anybody doing this should be aware of because it's powerful stuff. We thought it would be but we've been quite taken aback by the power literature can have over people's emotions.
> Writer in residence

Management

The writer in residence coordinated and managed the literature programme and reported to a line manager and to a management group which comprised the Governor of Inmate Activities, the Finance Director, a representative of South West Arts, the coordinator of the Writers in Prisons Network and Stephenson herself. The facilitators agreed the selection of texts and themes for discussion collectively and the course was run by Galbraith.

Timetable

Over the period 2000-3 there were eight 10-week courses, each taking place in prisoners' free association time, and one three-day intensive course run in response to participants' requests for more. Although participants often wished *Connections* was longer than 10 weeks, Galbraith felt the course's brief and intense nature was one of its strengths.

---

[30] Listeners are prisoners trained by the Samaritans.

Texts and issues

The facilitators had a pool of texts which they used to purse particular issues which included: *Deliverance* by James Dickey; *Made in Britain* by David Leland; *The Sea Wolf* by Jack London; *One Flew Over the Cuckoo's Nest* by Ken Kesey; *Of Mice and Men* by John Steinbeck; *Angela's Ashes* by Frank McCourt; *Alias Grace* by Margaret Atwood; *Oliver Twist* by Charles Dickens; and *Crime and Punishment* by Fyodor Dostoyevsky. On the first course the facilitators tried to plan ahead all the texts and discussion themes but they found that it was more useful to work flexibly and select texts and issues that followed on from those of previous sessions. The choice of text was issue-led first and foremost but there was also an element of chopping and changing.

> So it's also 'let's have a modern writer this week because we've had a couple of classics'. And we think about the writers themselves, it might be appropriate to do a black writer or a woman writer. Or if one week has been really in your face let's have one that's a bit lighter, *One Flew Over the Cuckoo's Nest* is a good one for that because it is an apparently lighter piece.
> Writer in residence

Other considerations

Everyone was expected to respect the confidentiality of discussions so that participants felt more willing to talk about their emotions and personal life and felt more confident that what they revealed would not be 'used' by others in the group.

Participants' final essays and a report on each participant's attendance and involvement on the course went to Probation and these could be taken into account when making decisions about parole, licenses and tagging.

Recruitment of participants

Attendance was voluntary but participants were expected to attend all sessions. *Connections* was promoted through the prison magazine, flyers, word of mouth and staff mentioning it to people who they thought might be interested. One of the *Connections* facilitators, a principal prison officer who worked on the wings of the prison, played a key role in bringing the course to the attention of participants. In addition, one of the positive outcomes of having a long-running programme was that graduates themselves generated interest in the course; several of the 12 participants enrolling on the April 2002 course joined the course because friends recommended it.

The most common reason participants gave for joining the course was the positive influence completing it might have on their parole. However, participants also referred to wanting to get their 'brains back in gear', being attracted by the 'literature side of it' and their hopes that they would benefit from doing the course.

Project activity

In the month prior to the April 2002 course, the *Connections* team visited Boston to observe the variety of approaches used on the *Changing Lives Through Literature* programme. They returned to HMP Channings Wood eager to try some fresh approaches and implemented some new ideas in the very first session of the course where the group discussed Irvin Welsh's *The Shooter* and a poem, *Mother to Son*.

> We'd sat in on one session in Boston which started off right in there – discussion and reading – instead of what we had been doing [in the first session] which was general, this is what we do and have a cup of tea, does anybody have any questions, a bit namby-pamby really. We tried a different approach and launched straight into it and they really rose to it and the discussion took off, very powerful discussion.
> Course leader

Each week participants were asked to prepare for the following week's session by reading a selected text. In each session the group discussed the text they had read and how it related to them. For example, *Oliver Twist* was used to discuss manipulation and *Of Mice and Men* formed the focus of discussion about relationships and dreams. Stephenson also arranged for a theatre group to visit the prison and perform *Macbeth* – this was then used as vehicle for discussing greed, ambition and guilt within the *Connections* group.

The facilitators looked for texts that were powerful and they expected quality from the discussions.

> That's what I meant about focus in discussion, it's not a gossip session, they're there to talk about issues. Really, I want them to go away buzzing and they do, they very often complain they can't sleep.
> Writer in residence

The course leader structured discussions more than in previous courses and this appeared to work well.

> Before we'd say 'okay, what do you think of that?' The issues came from them. Now it's more focused. So this week was about greed and ambition and next week it's going to be about what we do with the guilt. We wouldn't have done that before, we'd just have said, 'okay, what do you think of Macbeth?' just to see what would happen.
> Writer in residence

Both facilitators and participants felt that the group dynamics took around three weeks to settle and that the group emerged as a supportive one where individuals could hold different views and challenge one other. Interviews with participants suggested they entered the first session with mixed emotions - many were feeling 'positive' but also 'anxious', 'nervous' and in some cases 'suspicious' but these feelings abated as the course progressed.

> ... but things were established after about three weeks. Up until then, there was a bit of caution, a bit of tennis, ulterior motives, by that I mean trying to impress, all sorts... I could watch that all day!
> Participant

> The most positive thing about the course was the change within the group itself. Day one people were very, very apprehensive and suspicious of the fact there was an officer sitting there. They were concerned of what the motives behind it were. As the group went on over the ten weeks or so you saw people relaxing and trusting the rest of the group and feeling they could speak more openly. That was really good.
> Participant

Outcomes

Attendance figures
Seven of the 12 participants beginning the course completed it. One dropped out following the first session, two left after three or four weeks, one got early release and another attended all sessions apart from the final session (attendance of which is compulsory in order to complete the course).

Discussion of stories, characters and self-reflection
People generally enjoyed having a range of texts, discussing a variety of different topics and the mix of different views.

> The subjects were all different. One week to the next was never the same. They [the Connections team] got it right at that level.
> Participant

All six of the participants interviewed at the end of the course felt they had had freedom to develop their own ideas and five out of the six said they had sometimes felt challenged (in a good way) to try new things or think in a different way.

Throughout the course there were examples of participants identifying with fictional characters, situations or emotions – these revealed themselves in the discussions and in the notes and final essays written by participants. Most of the men felt there was a time where either a text, or something someone had said within one of the subsequent discussions, had 'hit a raw nerve' or been particularly enlightening. The thoughts and feelings that had been triggered were deeply felt to the extent that they had continued to think about things even after they had left sessions.

> The reading puts you in the area and triggers lots of ideas and different thoughts – I mean everyone has different views on different things and it's your response to those different thoughts and how you think about them, as well as the reading itself. Sometimes the reading is very relevant to the individual and sometimes it's the comments and the area you find yourself in.
> Participant

> When a raw nerve was hit and I disclosed things from my past that really affected me they [the Therapeutic Community] would help me. I left, at least seven times out of ten, I left those sessions carrying a lot in my mind, just chewing over, I left with so much in my head relating to me that I'd sit back and go over it again and work out why a piece of text that managed to develop into me, going to places that it did. It was partly the flow of the group and not anyone in particular taking it a step deeper each time throughout a session to a point where either myself or someone else would sort of connect what the last person said….
> Participant

> But the **most** significant thing was right at the end of the course and we'd done all our own reports, the last night we were there. We were asked to answer a couple of questions one of the facilitators wrote for us and one bloke said something that was so profound it kept me awake for nights afterwards just thinking about it because it was so relevant.
> Participant

The facilitators regarded the course as the best that had occurred so far. This was felt to be due to several factors: three or four of the men came prepared from the first session to really 'jump in at the deep end'; the facilitators using some of the approaches they had observed in Boston; and also the course having been running for two years.

> This was probably one of the best groups we have had… and that was partly because I think that institutionally it takes quite a long time for a course like this to bed down. And I think now although people bring various levels of expectations to the course, I think that the fact is you can cut through a lot of nonsense quite quickly because on the whole the course has become known.
> Course leader

Broadened experience of literature and of the arts
Generally, all participants were book readers prior to *Connections* but in many cases people's reading had been restricted to a particular genre, such as thrillers or horror, or to books that supported their studies. As a result of the course, all six participants interviewed at the end of the course felt they had more appreciation of literature - they now read in a different way and for some, the experience had fired up an interest in reading a wider range and different types of books. All six were planning on continuing their involvement in literature.

> It's changed me a little bit. It changed my perception on things a little and, the words are difficult, but sort of put me on a higher plane in literature and other circles as well. It's hard to find the words. Rather than being on a Peter and Jane level it took me above that! To the fact of liking different types of literature that I otherwise wouldn't have even tried. I wouldn't have gone near them – not a chance… It's changing stuff that I'm reading now. I only read Stephen King sort of stuff, that was my sort of level, but now I will pick up other stuff I'm not familiar with.
> Participant

> The way I read has definitely changed. It adds more substance to the characters you sort of read the characters in a book in a different way now, or I do. It's hard to describe. When I used to read it was flat if you like and now there's substance to them.
> Participant

Four felt their views about the arts had become more positive as a result of *Connections*; there was no doubt that the performance of *Macbeth* contributed to this change of perspective. Prior to the prison performance, several participants had had no or very little previous experience of Shakespeare, or of theatre more generally, and the theatre group's visit was viewed as one of the highlights.

Enjoyment
All six men enjoyed the course. Five of the six said they would like to be involved in more projects like *Connections*; the one who said he would not, had enjoyed the course and found it beneficial, but the experience at times had been so demanding and draining that he would not want to do it again.

> It was a very enjoyable experience. If I ever had a chance to do anything like that again either inside or outside prison, I'd seriously consider it.
> Participant

All six participants felt the course had helped them express themselves, five felt it had broadened their horizons, and three felt it had improved their quality of life.

> It's opened my eyes to some different areas that I've never been involved in before. How can I put it? I've never been near that kind of environment

for learning so that's changed my views on that a little bit. It's changed my views on the way you can learn. It's broadened my horizons.
Participant

If you do a little course like that and get something as big as that one play and understanding it and you've then got the choice to go on and watch a few more Shakespeare's and see what you can get from that. Then it's improved your life somewhere hasn't it?
Participant

Evaluation

Participants completed 'how I see myself' forms at the start and at the end of the course; these could then be compared. They also wrote essays at the end of *Connections* on how the course had changed their perspectives of both themselves and literature.

After the project

The writer in residence had always tried to build in measures for ensuring projects continued by involving staff and volunteers who might run things in her absence. However, *Connections* ceased following the departure of Stephenson and several of the facilitators at HMP Channings Wood. Part of the reason may be that the project was not accredited and did not contribute to the education department's performance targets. However, two of the *Connections* team (Stephenson and Galbraith) have gone on to pilot a programme of projects based on the HMP Channings Wood model. The programme, funded by the Paul Hamlyn Foundation, has been rolled out in a range of criminal justice settings. The pilots are going well and all venues have been interested in continuing the initiative.

In terms of sustaining activity for *Connections* graduates, one initiative that worked well was holding an intensive three-day course focusing on *Othello*.

Good practice

- The flexibility of the programme was one of its strengths – it can be run in different ways, with different types of offenders and with different age groups. In addition, the programme can incorporate different types and styles of writing (from poems to novels) and other artforms (such as drama or film)
- Having a pool of texts covering a range of different types of writer and issues
- Having tried pre-planning a course, the *Connections* team found that being flexible worked well because it enabled them to select texts and themes that followed on from previous sessions

- It was useful to have someone on the team with counselling skills. Stephenson also ensured prisoners had access to emotional support outside the sessions via the Listeners scheme
- The democratic forum worked well. One of the things participants liked was that there was no right or wrong answer and that everyone's view was valid
- Security issues were handled by having a supportive prison officer on the facilitator team. Having supportive wing staff was also helpful in terms of recruiting participants
- One of the benefits of having a long-running programme was that the course had time to 'bed down' institutionally and that there were course graduates who promoted the course amongst their peers
- Trust needed to be established in order for participants to feel able to talk about personal issues. Ensuring everyone signed up to a contract of confidentiality helped contribute towards this

Learning points

- There were certain oversights in the original budget. For example, the writer in residence felt it would have been a nice gesture to give at least one book to each participant at the end (this was built into the Paul Hamlyn pilots)
- The writer in residence had assumed the prison would view facilitators' time on the project as counting against their job. Those embarking on similar projects would be advised to check the situation in their institution
- The writer in residence felt that one of the weaknesses of *Connections* was that it was only accessible to those with literacy skills. By making audiotapes it might be possible for those who lack literacy skills to benefit from the course. Again, there would be a budgetary implication
- The team found that being direct in making the bridge between texts and how they relate to individuals worked well
- One participant on the April 2002 course adversely affected the dynamics of the group. One of the facilitators spoke to the individual concerned and the problem stopped for a while before returning. The course leader, on reflection, wished the staff team had dealt more quickly and effectively with the issue
- The course leader felt that the final essays were the weakest part of the programme – they tended to be conclusion-like and because they went to Probation participants were wary of being too revealing. He felt there would be value in sitting down with individual participants to discuss the task – people required more one-to-one support in the task
- Some participants (but not all) felt the repeated assurances regarding the confidentiality of discussions were 'overdone' and said they had not known the final essay would be circulated around the group. These issues were discussed openly in the final session and taken on board by the staff team

Further information

Publications

Stephenson, M. (2002). *Connections with Changing Lives Through Literature: Report following visit to Boston, Massachusetts comparing methodology and responses in the US and in Britain*. Welshpool: Writers in Prison Network, unpublished. Available from Writers in Prison Network, PO Box 70, Welshpool SY21 0WB.

Waxler, R. & Troustine, J. (eds) (1999). *Changing Lives Through Literature*. USA: University of Notre Dame Press. Available from Notre Dame Press, Notre Dame, IN 46556, USA.

A.1.2: Model 3 project – Eastern Touring Agency and Mercury Theatre

Summary

Organisations: Eastern Touring Agency (ETA)[31], Cambridge and Mercury Theatre, Colchester[32]

Activity: the project included two four-week residencies for young offenders aged 16-18 years; the creation and running of *Common Ground*, a pathway drama group for graduates of the residencies; work with a variety of community groups; training; a conference; and a small follow-up participatory project

Mercury Theatre artists (2001 residency): Adrian Stokes, director, and two actors, Mary Seymour and Ignatius Anthony

Budget: £53,714. The New Audience Award amounted to £42,000 – the Mercury Theatre received £24,300 and ETA received £17,700. The additional funds came from North Essex Youth Offending Team (NEYOT), Essex Drugs Action Team and the Mercury itself, and were used to enhance the work with community groups

Dates: the Arts Council research focused on the four-week residency which took place from 18 June to 13 July 2001 and culminated with the cast performing their play, *Landed*, in the Mercury Theatre Studio

Participants: young offenders in North Essex

Arts Council research: interviews with the three participants who completed the 2001 residency and two who completed the pilot residency in 2000, the director and actors, staff from ETA and NEYOT; observation

Outputs

- seven young offenders completed the summer projects (the residencies were completed by three of the four participants who started the 2001 project and four of the seven who started the 2002 project)
- each of the groups worked with a director and professional actors (and in the second year a dancer) to devise, rehearse and perform a play
- the resulting plays, *Landed* and *The Trouble with Kids*, were each performed once at a local day centre and once at Mercury Theatre Studio. A total of 200-240 people saw the performances
- two people took up training opportunities connected with the residencies
- 95 people attended the *Out of the Tick Box* conference and the subsequent online debate generated 359 views and 21 replies

The model 3 project comprised a broad programme of work. The Arts Council research focused on the 2001 summer residency in which three young offenders worked with a director and two professional actors (and a graduate from the pilot residency who was there in a training capacity) to create a play. Their play,

---

[31] In July 2003 ETA was renamed Momentum Arts. For the most part this case study refers to the organisation as ETA as most of the project took place before the name change.

[32] This was one of the model 3 partnerships set up by the Arts Council. See Chapters 1 and 6 of *The art and inclusion* Research report 35 (Jermyn, 2004) for further information.

Landed, followed the fortunes of two families, one a local family and the other a family of refugees. It was performed to a group of older people at a local day centre and to an invited audience in Mercury Theatre Studio.

Organisations: ETA (now Momentum Arts) and The Mercury Theatre

ETA developed as a regional organisation that aimed to nurture new audiences for the arts in the Eastern region, working primarily with venues and touring companies. Before the start of the model 3 project, ETA had been changing its portfolio and developed a major strand of work focusing on social inclusion as part of an A4E programme called The Creative Promoter. In July 2003, ETA was renamed Momentum Arts, to reflect its change of direction and its four programme areas: The Diversity Programme; The Initiatives Programme; The Promoter's Network (a development of ETA's original remit of supporting venues); and the Inclusion and Regeneration Programme.

The Mercury Theatre is a relatively unusual venue in that there is a commitment at director and chief executive level to community work. However, Adrian Stokes, Associate Director, felt that although there has been an increasing synergy between artistic and education priorities there was still work to be done to embed community work into the long-term artistic vision of the whole organisation. The theatre delivers a comprehensive range of work in and with the community and schools; much of it is delivered by the company's actors and attests to the theatre's belief that the actors who work in the community should be the same actors seen on its stage.

Aims and objectives

The model 3 project had a number of objectives which included: to select an artist to take up a training placement with the Mercury; to evaluate the residency; to assist the Mercury devise and fundraise for future work with the placement artist; and to foster relationships between venues and artists committed to working with socially excluded groups. Other planned activity focused on:

- evaluation, monitoring and dissemination
- research (assessing the viability of social inclusion work in a selected group of venues and researching possible partnerships)
- marketing/audience development

The Mercury Theatre also set aims for each of the pieces of work it delivered as part of the model 3 project.

Residency aims and objectives

The Mercury Theatre first piloted a summer project for young offenders in 2000, an initiative which involved Colchester Borough Council and NEYOT. Building on the foundations laid down by the pilot, the aims of the 2001 and 2002 residencies were to: work with young offenders; research, devise and perform a play; and create work of truth and meaning.

Stokes felt that clear aims and objectives assisted the whole process of delivering a project: 'we're clearly saying, we're going to have a play at the end of this and you're going to contribute to it, you're going to help devise it, you're going to get up and do it'. NEYOT viewed the initiative as something that could help the team address the needs of young people with a view to preventing further offending; it regarded it as part of the armoury it has at its disposal.

> No one thing can stop a person offending but it gives them a real opportunity. It's about discipline, relationships, trust, building self-esteem… you're important and if you're not there, you let people down. It's probably the first time people have wanted them to be there. It turns some of their values on their heads.
> Project partner

Project planning and management

Research and development
Prior to the model 3 project, ETA and the Mercury had had a relationship that operated at a number of different levels over a number of years; for example, the theatre had, in association with Theatre Centre, provided the model for The Creative Promoter. A key interest of ETA was in disseminating to other venues what was learned from the Mercury's social inclusion work. ETA and the Mercury Theatre therefore developed an idea that would involve the Mercury delivering a summer residency for young offenders and ETA using that as a training opportunity for an artist. Both partners also wanted to develop broader programmes involving work in the community, training, research, evaluation, marketing and audience development.

Recruitment of artists for the 2001 residency
The work with young offenders was part of a larger residency in which teams of practitioners worked with young people in schools and colleges locally. The company's actors participated in a training week prior to the residency and subsequently two actors were selected to work on the young offenders project.

Management
The New Audiences award was split between the two partners; £24,300 was spent directly on work delivered by the Mercury and £17,000 was spent on work led by ETA such as the conference, artist's training placement and work with venues. Both partners felt the model 3 project was a valuable exercise:

> From Momentum's point of view we have learnt from the Mercury, from their models of working, and have disseminated this project as a model of

good practice to others we have met and worked with. For us, it was a valuable experiment that built on previous work with the Mercury.
Project partner

However, ETA and the Mercury felt there was less joint ownership of the project than either would have liked. ETA recognised it had been unable to be proactive in supporting the training and residency at the Mercury due to changes of personnel within ETA and time being allocated to Family Friendly work.[33] Therefore, additional time was spent later on working with Stokes to ensure the conference was as partnership-based as possible. The partnership covered the design and content of the conference as well as its evaluation, documentation and publicity; both partners felt it was a well coordinated and successful day.

Recruitment of participants for the residency

The recruitment of young people was carried out by NEYOT in the months leading up to the residencies. Doug Rodway, Head of NEYOT, described the young people he worked with as people who had been through the system:

> … they've been told they can't do anything, that they're useless, there's alienation within family and school, truanting, getting into trouble, a destructive school life. They've been through the system, social services, Children and Family Consultation and so on.
> Project partner

The young people YOTs encounter will often have a number of problems which need to be addressed, which is why the teams are made up of representatives from the Probation Service, health, education, drug and alcohol misuse and so on. NEYOT held team meetings to discuss the young people and their needs and tried to match people to the project that they felt would benefit them and that they were available to attend. Those that participated in the 2001 residency were a mix of people who were on pre-court final warnings and those on community orders. Eight young people met with Stokes and a participant from the 2002 residency to talk about the project; four attended in the first week and three completed the project.

One of the things that attracted participants to the project was the drama focus (all had an interest in drama/performance and two had studied it at school) but the effect that doing the project can have on the length of people's supervision orders was also a major motivating factor.

> I was enthusiastic. Firstly, it shortens my supervision order but also I really enjoy performing.
> Participant

---

[33] Key staff at ETA who had initiated the model 3 project left the organisation before it ended. This also impacted on the project timetable.

They told me I had to do a 12-week Prince of Edinburgh scheme or whatever it's called. Then they told me about this. At first I thought I was being stitched up but then I met Adrian and I thought it wouldn't be too bad.
Participant

Activity

The key activities delivered through the model 3 project were: two summer residencies for young offenders; the setting up and running of Common Ground theatre group; work with a variety of community groups (including North Essex Pupil Referral Unit, adults with learning difficulties, young people at risk which included a devised piece for Essex Drugs Action Team, a women's literacy group, work in a local secondary school and some work in a special school); training; a conference; and a small follow-on participatory project.

The Arts Council research focused on the 2001 residency in which a group of young offenders worked with actors to research, devise and perform a play in a period of four weeks. During the first week, project participants and the actors played games and exercises structured primarily for participation. Over the second and third weeks the focus changed to devising material that could be used in the play, *Landed*, after which stress was placed on rehearsal and getting prepared for performance. Participants' attendance in the first two weeks in particular fluctuated.[34] It was in the third week that Stokes noted that 'a more disciplined approach to content and form emerged. Participants could see the shape of the play emerging and began seriously to engage with it'.

In the final week the play was performed in a day centre for older people on the Wednesday morning and to an invited audience in the Mercury Theatre Studio the following evening. On the final day the group attended a debrief where they talked about the process, received certificates and signed programmes for one another. Stokes felt that meeting again post-performance was important: 'through it there is a coming down and preparation for the real world'.

Outcomes

Devise, create and perform a play
Participants and the Mercury team achieved their objective to research, devise and perform a play in both the 2001 and 2002 residencies. The plays, *Landed* and *The Trouble with Kids*, were generated from the young people's ideas, from improvisations, from research, games and exercises. For example, in the 2001

---

[34] Daily attendance was required except in circumstances where people had valid reasons for not attending, such as court appearances. NEYOT played an important role in ensuring participants reached rehearsals and chasing up any 'no-shows'.

residency one participant told a story about an asylum seeker who had stolen someone's purse, the group thought that was interesting and it prompted the idea for their play, *Landed*, which explored refugees' experiences. Other specific examples of material generated by participants included the use of 'gibberish' to create a scene and the use of frozen images which had been generated through visual exercises.[35] The participants also conducted some research eg they interviewed older people in a local day centre to find out about how life in the past compared with life now. The process was directed by Stokes who used his skills to structure the material and the resulting plays were performed to audiences in the final week.

Participant outcomes

Art and creative skills
All three participants who completed the 2001 residency felt they had developed arts/creative skills and learned to think more creatively/use their imagination; all had been involved in a devising process and developed movement, voice and other skills needed to perform the play to a high standard. Two had felt positive about the arts before the project but one said he felt 'a bit better about them now, a bit more positive'. All three participants expressed an interest in continuing with drama in some way (and one of them did so through *Common Ground*).

Pride
The participants said they were proud of what they and the group had achieved. Stokes believed that for some, seeing the project through to the end was in itself a major achievement requiring discipline and commitment. One of the 2001 participants described how he had never finished anything - he felt proud that he had regularly attended rehearsals and seen the project through to its conclusion.

All identified the performance as a high point; the audience, which included participants' family and friends, YOT workers, Mercury Theatre actors and ETA staff, was very positive and responsive.

> Doing the play. It was pucker in front of the audience. At the time I was thinking I'll have a laugh and bunk off today but I didn't. It went perfectly. Participant

> Participant 1:[of the performance] It was wicked, I want to do it again. Everyone did really well.
> Participant 2: I'm really sad the four weeks is over. I really loved it. I'd have liked to have seen it from the audience perspective.

---

[35] Gibberish was an exercise that some participants particularly enjoyed and involved them having conversations using gibberish rather than words.

108

Participant 3:The look on my face says everything. I didn't stop smiling all evening.

The Thursday evening performance was remarkable for its commitment and discipline. Confidence visibly increased during the show, sufficiently for some members of the cast to start taking risks with each other and the material, within the proper context of scenes. The audience were clearly appreciative of the quality of work the company had achieved.
Director, Landed evaluation report

Confidence
All three participants felt they had become more confident as a result of the project and that it had helped them feel good about themselves. Two participants from the pilot residency similarly felt that the experience had helped them develop confidence, and that that confidence had stayed with them. Stokes believed the confidence was physically visible, something that was echoed by one participant:

> I used to slouch lots. It got up my confidence a lot, I think that was the main thing. It wasn't a full-blown play but at the end of the day it was a play at the Mercury Theatre and I thought wow.
> Participant

Group working
All three felt they were part of a team, that they had learned to trust others in the group and that they had become more committed to achieving group goals. Over the course of the four weeks the dynamics within the group changed as the day of the performances grew closer – attendance improved, one participant changed his habits outside of the project because he was worried he would not remember his lines, and in the final run-throughs the group self-policed.

> I enjoyed working with the team, I cannot emphasise how much I've enjoyed the project.
> Participant

> The gradual acceptance of responsibility both for the content of the play and to each other is a real strength, because it depends on trusting others, which for some is not a familiar sensation.
> Director

Enjoyment
All three of the 2001 residency participants enjoyed the project 'a lot'. The participants had particularly enjoyed 'getting to know everyone', 'putting together the characters', 'working alongside the professional actors' and the audience's reaction to their performance. The process was described as fun and contrasted against participants' negative experiences of school.

I loved every bloody minute.
Participant

They didn't treat you like students and kids, they don't refer to you as 'right, you shouldn't be talking'... they talk to you like you're an equal, they won't snigger and laugh at you. They kind of capture you – they make you want to do it.
Participant

[What enjoyed the most] The opportunity to work with professional actors. Having the, what's the word? having the honour of working with them. The whole opportunity really.
Participant

It's much better fun that at school. I hated school. I was always messing about, in every class. They'd go on and I'd be right I'm going to make it worse and then I'd swap schools and I'd clown around, become one of the boys, and start over.
Participant

Rodway felt one of the key benefits of the project was the positive focus it provided for participants.

The type of thing they say to case workers before and after are different. They're far more able to articulate feelings, genuinely more able to look at their lives in context. I've done something, it's been exciting, where can I go with that? Rather than negative, why have I offended again? why did I do that? It is something positive to hang on to. It's something we need to work on at the end of the scheme so they have something they can channel into.
Project partner

Patterns of offending
The young people participating in the residencies were characterised as medium to high risk of reoffending. Following the residencies of 2000 and 2001 NEYOT noted that some young people had stopped offending, some stopped for the duration of the residency and the offending of others slowed down. At the time of writing there had been four summer residencies; the YOT confirmed that over the four years the level of reoffending for participants has been 30% (compared to 68% among the medium to high risk group that have not participated in the residency).

Some participants described the project in life-changing terms; for example, one went on to study drama and is a workshop assistant at the theatre. However, there was also an example of a participant who was a prolific offender who stopped offending while he was doing the project and returned to old patterns once the project finished (behaviour which Rodway felt should not be regarded as failure but a demonstration of how valued he felt on the scheme). Reflecting on the pilot and the 2001 residency, Stokes felt the results confirmed that the project worked best 'for people who are looking for the out – even if they weren't able to identify what that way out was'.

Other

Two of the group said they felt physically 'better', as one put it 'usually I stay in bed late but I was getting up early, I wanted to get in' and all three felt more motivated. One participant felt the project had helped him with his anger.

Establishing the *Common Ground Theatre Group*

Once participants had completed the summer residency, what next? As one project partner noted, 'it's like they've come in from the cold and they're turned out again. Some will just say that was good and get on with things but for some the intensity of it opens up a new avenue and that is then taken away'. In an attempt to address this Stokes founded *Common Ground*, a pathway drama group for graduates of the summer residencies. His ambition was to establish a group with a burgeoning reputation so that the group itself would become a catalyst for people wanting to join the summer residencies.

The group started in September 2001 and three people attended the weekly sessions regularly. However, the number of participants was too few to sustain the group when anyone was absent or late and it proved difficult to increase the size of the group because several of the participants in subsequent residencies were from outside the Colchester area. The Mercury has not abandoned its aspiration and is developing additional youth theatres away from the theatre site; summer participants will be prioritised as members. The theatre also maintains contact with participants, often through the actors who have worked with them who invite participants to see them in productions.

Training opportunities

Training opportunities were offered in three ways:

- **training for Mercury staff**: in both 2001 and 2002 the theatre's actors and trainees attended a training week to prepare them for the residencies. It was felt that the aims of the week were achieved; it established a coherent Mercury Theatre ethos and practice. In addition the theatre's staff were provided with equal opportunities and social inclusion training
- **apprenticeship**: a participant from the pilot residency worked as an apprentice on the 2001 residency. Most of the aims and objectives set for the traineeship were achieved. When *Common Ground* floundered, the money

which was originally earmarked for the theatre group was used to provide the trainee with a longer-term placement

- **artist's training placement**: a dance artist, Sam Dawn, was selected to take up the training placement on the 2002 residency. The experience provided her with an opportunity to work in a new setting and with practitioners from a different artform. She went on to set up a follow-up project, coordinated by Momentum Arts, in partnership with Haverhill Town Council and Haverhill On-Track, involving young people at risk[36]

The work placement confirmed its value as a training method and the Mercury hopes to continue offering such opportunities to artists. The apprenticeship was viewed by Stokes as an example of how, with the right opportunities, participants can be sustained in their determination to change their lives.

Out of the Tick Box conference

The project's objectives concerned with disseminating findings and fostering best practice were achieved primarily through the delivery of a conference, *Out of the Tick Box*. The conference, held in November 2002, was attended by 95 delegates and focused on practice, progression and partnerships in the area of arts and social inclusion. It brought together case studies exploring good practice and showcased the Mercury Theatre's summer residency. Feedback was positive with 81% of 27 respondents saying they would be likely to follow up issues raised on the day.

The mix of people attending the day was regarded as one of the highlights; there were representatives from a wide range of agencies but also many artists and project participants (some of whom were involved in the case studies). With more time, more work could have been undertaken to involve the young people from the residencies in the conference planning. Nevertheless, project participants were actively involved in the day and this was felt to be a positive outcome.

The conference enabled ETA to develop its changing focus to work with a wider range of partners. ETA reported that many middle-scale venues and local authorities with no previous links to ETA attended the conference and were interested in developing social inclusion work.

The day stimulated debate which continued on the Heroic website, ETA's online discussion board. By the end of January 2003, the contribution of one of the speakers, Brian Belton, Senior Lecturer at YMCA George Williams College in London, had generated 359 views, 21 replies and spawned two new discussion strands. A rapporteur submitted a report on the day and ETA plan to use this and other material to create an accessible report for dissemination.

---

[36] This was part-funded through the model 3 partnership.

Research and marketing

A large number of objectives were set which centred on developing social inclusion work in venues and marketing (see section 5.3).

ETA approached some venues about developing social inclusion work but none expressed an interest in taking the idea further and because of changes in staffing at the organisation the idea was not pursued. There were a variety of potential reasons why no expressions of interest were received: venues could not take on such a commitment because of existing commitments; the work did not fit well with venues' planned programme; and venues could not necessarily work to the model 3 timetable. ETA felt that venues needed time to build capacity, understanding and resources in order to develop work in the area of social inclusion. Some venues were simply reluctant to take this path, as one of the project partners explained: 'there has to be a will within organisations. If the will isn't there, if you're not coming from the same place then it's difficult. The work isn't for everyone – there has to be an integrity to it'.

On reflection, ETA felt that more discussion should have been held with venues before the proposal was developed to gauge interest. This has partly been addressed since the model 3 project by Momentum Arts in the development of its Creative Communities programme with the Promoters Network. An extensive consultation process took place and venues were encouraged to identify areas of priority which included working with young people in inclusive settings. This response, it believes, was partly due to the nature of the consultation and partly about the changed socio-political landscape.

In terms of the marketing objectives, it was decided at the point of new staff picking up the project, with only a few months remaining, to focus on marketing the conference and producing a report – shifting the focus to dissemination of best practice. The conference focused on practice, progression and partnerships but some of the breakout sessions such as Freeform Arts Trust and Theatre Resource showed examples of good practice in marketing.

Evaluation

Evaluation was built into the day-to-day delivery of the residencies and was one of the subjects covered in the training weeks. Several methods were used:

- the actors at the end of each day discussed what had and had not worked and planned for the following day – notes of these discussions were kept
- there were regular 'catch-ups' with participants to gauge feelings and views
- during the debrief day the cast broke into small groups and made a note of what they had done over the four weeks and how they had felt
- the cast, director and technician completed feedback forms

- the artist who did the training placement in 2002 completed a written report
- the Mercury Theatre had an assessment meeting which all actors attended

The conference was evaluated through use of feedback forms and there was also an evaluation meeting held towards the end of the project where the partners reflected on what had been achieved and the lessons learned.

In both organisations an emphasis was placed on individual practitioners and staff sharing the lessons they have learned from the project with others within their respective organisations. Lessons learned have also been shared through an article in *Arts Professional* and though ETA's day-to-day dealings with artists, venues and policy makers.

After the project

Both ETA and the Mercury Theatre are committed to developing social inclusion work as part of their core activities. The summer project with young offenders is continuing and the Mercury Theatre is committed to opening up training opportunities for artists wishing to develop their skills in this type of work. The Mercury has further developed the extent of its relationships with the community, including the Pupil Referral Unit and Youth Service, with an emphasis on young people at risk. However, Stokes noted that to do the work properly, a high staff to participant ratio is needed and this makes such work expensive:

> The model 3 funding is finished and no alternative funding has been found and no clear routes to finding it established. There are several routes for setting up new projects – trusts, foundations etc, but for the continuance of established and effective models of good practice?
> Project partner

ETA felt the project enabled it to strengthen networks and raised awareness of its work in this area. The establishment of an Inclusion and Regeneration Manager post was felt to have happened partly as a result of the model 3 project.

Good practice

- Both the Mercury Theatre and Momentum have incorporated the practice and learning from the Model 3 project into their ongoing work
- The planning of the conference worked to ensure that participants from projects highlighted on the day were able to attend. The fact that this was achieved was a success and meant that a range of experiences and viewpoints were presented at the conference
- The training week successfully prepared the actors, some of whom were new to this area of work, for the residencies
- Involvement of a previous year's participant in the recruitment phase and delivery of the project (via a traineeship) was felt to be a very positive

114

development; her presence was an excellent bridge between participants and the company
- The model of participants and professional actors working alongside one another was an effective one
- The project was properly resourced and the costs of food, childcare and taxis were included in the budget. While these added to project costs they were felt to be necessary for success eg the provision of food enabled participants to build energy, the provision of a taxi ensured that people got to rehearsals
- Creating something of high quality generated a real sense of achievement amongst participants and because of the process participants felt a strong sense of ownership of the final product; it was their play
- The project was part of the Mercury's ongoing commitment to working with the community. There are plans to continue delivering the residency for young offenders and the Mercury has also attempted to create progression routes
- In response to participant feedback in the pilot 2000 residency, YOT staff were more actively involved in the 2001 residency
- The debrief was a useful vehicle for providing project closure and obtaining feedback
- Evaluation was built into the project and the resources were made available

Learning points

- On reflection, ETA felt it had been very ambitious when setting their objectives – more time would be needed to achieve them
- ETA has established that there are many venues in the region that have identified young people as a priority and are genuinely interested in developing work with this group but many need more strategic support to successfully achieve this
- Momentum Arts now seeks to resource work across the organisation rather than having projects run by one person only
- Key learning points from the conference included:
    o questioning the value of parachuting into people's or communities' lives without having adequate resources or partnerships to provide progression
    o placing creativity at the heart of the process
    o giving appropriate support and value to the experiences of participants
    o being aware of individual learning styles
- Learning points emerging from the 2001 residency included:
    o on occasion taxis failed to turn up to collect participants - this was identified as something that needed to be addressed in future residencies
    o the need to build in more studio time
- Some participants felt the impact of the project ending more than others and the YOT was considering how it could help in this respect. Certainly the intervention of YOT following the project would seem to be key in not only

supporting the participants through the 'low' but also in redirecting participants' energy and commitment

Further information

Websites
http://www.momentumarts.org.uk   Momentum Arts (formerly ETA)
http://www.heroic.uk.com   Heroic
http://www.mercurytheatre.co.uk   Mercury Theatre

A.1.3: Fashion and ID

Summary

Organisations: artworks-mk and Milton Keynes Gallery (MK G)[37]

Activity: photography and mixed media workshops based on identity leading to exhibitions of work

Commissioned artists: Malcolm Glover, photographer, and Christine Wilkinson, visual artist

Budget: £41,000. £35,000 from New Audiences Programme and £6,000 from Audiences mk

Dates: planning began in April 2001, outreach started in September and workshops were delivered from October through to December 2001. Participants' work was exhibited at MK G for two weeks during December 2001 and also on a market stall in central Milton Keynes and at Coffee Hall Arts Workshop

Participants: older people (aged 60 plus) and younger people (aged 12-18) living in Coffee Hall, Milton Keynes

Arts Council research: interviews with project partners and artists; observation

Outputs:

* 20 younger people and 10 older people had some level of participatory involvement in the project, 16-21 of these regularly attended workshops
* the artists delivered six outreach sessions and 21 workshops
* 20 participants exhibited their work at MK G and ten participants visited MK G for an evening reception and viewing of their work; it was their first visit to the gallery
* 529 people attended the MK G exhibition, over 150 shoppers stopped at the market stall and the participants' work was also installed in the windows of Coffee Hall Arts Workshop

Through *Fashion and ID*, artworks-mk and MK G hoped to develop understanding and awareness between older and younger people living in Coffee Hall, to obtain a greater knowledge about the groups' cultural needs and attitudes to fashion and identity, and to increase audiences of older and younger people.

Research was commissioned to learn about the two target groups and to inform the project; the marketing agency MAX (Marketing the Arts in Oxford) compiled statistical material about the social and economic profile of Coffee Hall and facilitated focus groups with residents.

Two artists were commissioned and they led a series of workshops in which participants used mixed media and photography to create life-sized images of

---

[37] This was one of the model 3 partnerships brokered by the Arts Council. Further information is provided in the Chapters 1 and 6. The partnerships were set up to test certain ways of working.

themselves and fantasy shoe sculptures. The participants' work was exhibited at MK G, on a market stall and in the windows of Coffee Hall Arts Workshop.

The artists also ran two workshops for staff at artworks-mk and at MK G to facilitate team building between staff across the two organisations.

Organisations

Artworks-mk is an organisation that supports and promotes participation, learning and development through arts and crafts activities, projects, and events in Milton Keynes. MK G opened in 1999 and is a purpose-built contemporary art gallery presenting between eight and 10 free exhibitions a year. Artworks-mk and MK G have a history of working together on education projects which are planned in partnership; typically these involve split-site school visits to MK G to see an exhibition and then to artworks-mk to undertake practical workshops linked to the exhibition.

Aims and objectives

The project aimed to establish an understanding of the cultural needs of socially excluded older and younger people in Coffee Hall and for artworks-mk and MK G to develop and create a participant-led project around the theme of fashion and identity. A number of objectives were set including:

- to research and develop a 12-month project at Coffee Hall, focusing on socially excluded older and younger residents
- to gain greater knowledge about older and younger people in Coffee Hall and their involvement and attitude to fashion and identity
- to contribute to the development of a healthy community through improved communications and understanding between older and younger people in Coffee Hall
- to work with marketing and evaluation specialists to improve data collection, audience development and evaluation practices
- for both organisations to increase audiences of older people (by 10%) and younger people (by 15%) through informed programming, education, communications and information during 2002
- for older and younger people to produce an interactive publication for wide distribution to inform similar communities about fashion and identity of people generations apart

There was also an objective that was derived from the ethos behind the model 3 partnerships that organisations would learn from each other.

The overall thrust of the project did not change – younger and older people explored identity through visual arts media. However, it was felt that it might have been valuable to review the aims and objectives as the project progressed.

I now think it would have been useful to revisit them once the project got started and say are we on target to meet these? What's still doable? What's not possible? Is there something else we could achieve from this project? Not to see them as absolutely set in stone at the beginning of the project but to say, we may change them and change them for a good reason.
Project partner

Project planning and management

Research

The partners commissioned MAX to collate statistical material about the social and economic profile of Coffee Hall and to conduct three focus groups. The groups aimed to explore attitudes to the visual arts in Milton Keynes, determine levels of enthusiasm for a participant-led project focused on the themes of fashion and identity, test creative ideas and explore the theme of 'younger and older'. Initially, the artist-led workshops were going to begin during MK G's exhibition *Look at Me: Fashion and Photography 1960 to the Present* which was seen as an excellent 'first-timers' exhibition and one to which younger and older people could all relate. However, project delays, which included the artist recruitment process taking longer than expected, meant this element of the project was lost, although the fashion and identity theme remained.

Recruitment of artists and other staff

Very early on in planning Malcolm Glover, photographer, was appointed as one of the project's artists and he helped develop the artists' brief. Originally, Glover's role was to work with MAX to explore concepts and ideas, recruit participants for the workshops (to be led by a fashion artist) and document the project.

There was a thorough recruitment process; both organisations were looking for specialist communication and engagement skills in the artists as well as a proven track record of working with excluded young people and it was also important that they recruited two artists who would be able to work together. It proved difficult to find an artist to lead the workshops but Christine Wilkinson, a visual artist, was recruited in July 2001.

When Wilkinson met Glover to discuss the project they agreed they would rather jointly deliver workshops. This decision was supported by artworks-mk and MK G, however, it meant that much of the project planning which had already taken place needed to be adapted to accommodate the artists' desire to work together and their view of the project. Pairing up minimised the vulnerability of the artist and improved the ratio of participants to adults. For the organisers this highlighted the importance of involving the artists at an early stage of project planning – a point of good practice which artworks-mk and MK G have now incorporated into project planning.

119

Artist 1: Very importantly it's two different disciplines and we both felt what a waste not to learn off each other really, as opposed to one running out on the streets looking for people and then passing it over to the other.
Artist 2: I didn't want to end up with someone documenting the project and somebody else producing the art, I felt it was much more productive to both be involved in the same creative process, working in different ways and then combining.

The artists felt the groups benefited from having two artists to work with and in hindsight it was felt that lone working with the younger age group would have been inappropriate given the needs of the group. They also felt working together benefited their professional practice.

It has been important for us to explore not only the way that two different forms can work together, but also attitudes to making work and approaches to participating practice. We have been quite fortunate that neither of us felt territorial about our own medium or about our approach to the project.
Artists [from artists' evaluation report]

It became clear in the second young people's workshop that it was a challenging and volatile group. The environment they were working in, an arts and crafts workshop with lots of rooms and hidden corners, compounded difficulties. The artists and project partners promptly recruited someone with a social work background to attend future sessions. A member of staff from either artworks-mk or MK G also attended sessions bringing the total staff complement in the young people's workshops to four adults. Although this increased the cost of each workshop, it was felt that this delivery 'team' was vital and should be established from the outset in future projects with challenging or volatile participants.

Management
Originally, project management was going to be shared equally between artworks-mk and MK G. However, as planning progressed MK G realised it would not be able to deliver the necessary hours required given its existing commitments and staff resources (a key member of staff was on maternity leave for a significant part of the project). This was addressed in a number of ways; for example, artworks-mk took on a bigger share of project management.

Artworks-mk was largely responsible for managing the outreach and workshop phase of the project and MK G managed the exhibition and market stall. The roles and responsibilities of artworks-mk and MK G were formally laid out in a partnership agreement which was drawn up before the workshops began – it broke the project down at task level and identified the individuals responsible for carrying out each task. This was useful in formalising who was doing what but both partners questioned the value of having such a detailed contract. On reflection, the partners felt it would have been beneficial for them to have spent more time planning how each organisation could benefit long-term from the project and the contribution each could make.

Timetable
The project, as originally planned in April 2001, was devised to tie in with the summer exhibition at MK G, *Look at Me: Fashion and Photography in Britain 1960 to the Present*. However, the project started later than planned; this was largely because the research commissioned to inform their plans took longer than expected due to the amount of primary research but also because of the time it took to recruit appropriately experienced artists. In a participant-led project the artists and organisations also had to respond flexibly to groups' needs and this impacted on the project timetable; as one project partner explained in an interim report on the project, 'the activity has needed to remain fluid in order to respond to change. Therefore, it has proved difficult to slot a project like this into specific exhibition timescales as originally planned'.

A later exhibition slot was booked and the summer exhibition was used to inspire *Fashion and ID*. Outreach and workshops began in October 2001 and the exhibition at MK G took place in December 2001.

Recruitment of participants

Older participants
Older participants were recruited from sheltered accommodation in Coffee Hall. The artists investigated working with other groups but these were ruled out because their members came from too wide a catchment area. The artists did some outreach work where they visited residents and chatted about photographs, fashion and identity. However, it proved difficult to establish a group who would attend sessions at the nearby Coffee Hall Arts Workshop – this was partly due to issues around illness and frailty but also a lack of confidence about making the move from familiar territory to a new space. Four older people regularly came to workshops but on reflection the artists felt that it might have been more productive to draw people in from other groups and to have delivered some sessions at the sheltered housing complex itself.

> Artist 1: We would have needed more time to go around some of the lunch clubs, maybe the bowls club, talked to people, pulled out single individuals and got them together as a group.
> Artist 2: The actual project would have worked because in the first two or three workshops where people were just talking, getting out their photo albums, talking about fashions, it was great. But you needed more time.
> Artists

Younger participants

The artists met with a local youth worker and told young people at the local youth club about the project. However, the artists noticed that there were many young people 'hanging around' outside the club (from which they were banned) and they proceeded to chat to them about the project – it was this group that became the main focus of the project. The artists successfully established a regular group of 17 young people who attended workshops. The artists sought advice from the participants themselves on what timings would suit them and where to advertise the project.

> Our approach to timing of sessions is part of the engagement process where people feel they have some negotiation power. Part of what we're thinking about is placing more and more of the agenda in the control of people taking part. We decided rather than saying 'the workshop is being held at this time', to do it the other way round and ask 'what suits you?'
> Artist

The artists also visited the main secondary school for the area and ran some sessions there which involved some of the young people from Coffee Hall. The engagement and retention of these excluded young people by the artists was a great success. It took particular skills and experience from Glover and Wilkinson to be able to do this so effectively.

Project activity

There were four main project areas: outreach; workshops; exhibition of work at MK Gallery, artwork-mk's Coffee Hall Arts Workshop and Central Milton Keynes Market; and the publication.

The artists' original plan was that participants would take, develop and print photographs and use those images to create a collage within a life-size profile of themselves. The idea of the profile outline was decided early on and worked well with the younger group in particular.

> We decided on a format that would be quite contained for them, that would give them structure that was based on themselves, so within that they could have freedom. Another thing was that the work would hang together as a group quite well.
> Artist

The younger group filled their life-size profiles with images taken from magazines and drawings (they preferred to keep the photographs they had taken). The group also created fantasy shoe sculptures.

The artists acknowledged that the older group did not necessarily produce much artwork but they were pleased with what happened and the journey individuals took. Four older people developed and printed photographs for the first time and one was an enthusiastic participator, taking photographs of young people on the estate and creating a life-size image of herself filled with photographs of places and people that made up her life.

The exhibition was regarded as a vital part of the project and both partners were pleased with the quality of the material produced. The artists accompanied the young people on their gallery visit and felt the experience had a big impact on them: 'they just wanted to stand next to their piece and soak it up'. The quality of the exhibition was high as was the finishing of the work; participants' work was treated with respect.

> It lifts it out of just having stuff that was on the floor and makes it very special. And it's the way myself as an artist I would present my work in the best way possible. That's the way I wanted to treat the work the kids made.
> Artist

The artists also exhibited participants' work on a market stall in Central Milton Keynes Market. Approximately 150 shoppers stopped to look at the shoes and images on the market stall. The public's comments were written down in a book and they illustrate how well received and good-humoured the public's response was – some even wanted to buy the shoes!

Outcomes

Plan and develop a project which focuses on socially excluded older and younger residents
The partnership was set up to explore a particular model of working and support organisational learning eg a large arts organisation (MK G) works with and learns from a smaller participatory arts organisation (artworks-mk). Both organisations felt that the initiative was successful in many respects and that many lessons were learned which have subsequently informed practice.

Project planning and management was shared and each partner tended to make use of the expertise it already had and play to its strengths. Both organisations found they had underestimated the amount of staff time required to manage the project; in the end each needed to 'do what they did best' even though this meant that there was not a significant amount of 'skills exchange' during the project. However, both artworks-mk and MK G felt they gained a greater awareness of each other's working practice, strengths and areas of expertise. In addition, staff from both organisations observed a workshop session and also gained valuable outreach experience on the market stall.

Artworks-mk and MK G are both based in Milton Keynes and have interests in promoting and developing the visual arts. However, they are different in many ways – in terms of their size, ways of working, aims and objectives and so on.

Each was aware that it had to allow for differences in each other's practice but at times this was challenging. For example, artworks-mk is a small organisation and their director took an active role in the project so decisions could be made very quickly, while MK G is a much larger organisation so decisions sometimes took longer to make because they needed to be approved by, or discussed with, the director or colleagues.[38]

Gain knowledge about older and younger people
The partners gained information about issues and needs when working with excluded groups of older and younger people and an insight into younger and older people's attitudes to fashion and identity because these were the themes explored in workshops and in the final artworks.

Improving understanding between older and younger people
Artworks-mk, MK G and the artists agreed that a longer time frame was needed to meet the intergenerational goals of the project. It was a task that had to be handled sensitively and only when both groups were ready. In addition, planning the project in partnership with an outside agency (for example, Milton Keynes Social Services, the Youth Service, Sure Start or Age Concern) would have contributed to this objective and to the long term success of the project.

Work with marketing and evaluation specialists to improve data collection, audience development and evaluation practices
Artworks-mk and MK G commissioned a piece of dedicated research to inform the project – neither organisation had worked with MAX prior to the project so have learned about their areas of expertise and methodology. Artworks-mk found the research conducted by MAX to be particularly useful because it provided statistics about an area of Milton Keynes in which it has an art workshop and qualitative data about residents' perceptions of the facility.

> Given normal budget restraints we have never experienced the value of project-based research until now. Working with MAX and using the information they gathered has been a different way of working for us and we are now great advocates of this working method.
> Project partner

MK G and the artists found the research of interest, but of less practical value because it focused on one particular estate in Milton Keynes. The research element of the project did highlight ways in which MK G was not collecting audience data as effectively as it could and practice has changed as a result of being involved in the project. For the artists, the research of most value in shaping the project was the research they themselves undertook.

---

[38] This issue was also present in some of the other partnership projects participating in the research programme eg Cardboard Citizens and the RSC.

For what they were asked they did an incredible job. But it didn't have much to do with the project. There were all these incredible statistics coming out but the kids we worked with we found on the streets. There were suggestions in there about where we could locate pensioners but we could have done that ourselves.
Artist

Increase audiences of older and young people
The artists worked with four older people who lived in sheltered accommodation and a group of 17 young people, many of whom had been 'banned' from mainstream youth work activities and were not attending school. However, from the start of the project it seems there was some misunderstanding about who would be targeted through the project. The artists understood their brief was to engage 'hard to reach' groups and young people who had been excluded from a youth club fitted that definition. However, MK G originally perceived the project as an audience development project with a geographically under-represented group (ie residents of Coffee Hall). Developing and supporting the small group of excluded young people to become an audience would have required much longer term financial and staff investment. Without dedicated funding and capacity for this purpose, this commitment was difficult to justify in a brand new gallery which needed to focus on building sustainable audiences in a cost-effective way.

It was the young people's first time in a gallery and one of the artists noted how 'their first experience of the professional art scene was coming to a specially arranged opening and seeing their own work looking terrific'. Similarly, the young people had not previously attended artwork-mk's workshops at Coffee Hall.

Interactive publication
A publication was initially planned for spring 2002. However, following discussions between the project partners it was felt that further audience development initiatives would be of greater benefit to both participants and partners. Both organisations ran further workshops with young people in the Coffee Hall area.

Evaluation

The partners and artists used a number of different techniques to monitor and evaluate the project including journals, an exhibition comments book and participant feedback questionnaires. However, one of the issues that impacted on the evaluation was the artists' feeling that outside visitors (including staff from artworks-mk or MK G) would be inappropriate in the early stages given the importance of establishing trust with these groups.

After the project

The question of what would happen when the project finished was a concern throughout the project. At the point where the project ended there was no definite plan, although artworks-mk was investigating ways of continuing work with the group. The cost of working with the young people in particular was an issue; the Arts Council investment enabled the project to take place but finding resources to sustain that work was difficult. In addition, MK G did not have the expertise or resources necessary to work with this group and develop them as an audience. The artists felt particularly uncomfortable that a solution was not found before they left the project:

> You've given kids an experience and then it's 'cheers, we're off now'. I question that. I personally think you shouldn't do that because they're let down again, that's what's happening all the time… All this money has been put into it, all the time we've put into this, and okay an exhibition has gone up but for me I feel this is the beginning. There's so much more you could do.
> Artist

Local agencies that might have had some interest in continuing activity were not actively involved from the start and staffing changes within youth services meant it was difficult to establish continuity and an effective working relationship. The partners now feel it is imperative that key organisations which have the capacity to sustain activity are engaged at the start of similar projects.

Artworks-mk worked with Faye Gilbert, film maker, to document the work of the young people – the video highlighted the pride the young people had in their work. As a result of the project artworks-mk is working with the National Children's Bureau on a project which has the support of social and youth services. The project will engage young people across the city in creative activities with a view to informing decision makers of their views and needs.

MK G has continued to work with Coffee Hall's main secondary school, an organisation with which it renewed contact during *Fashion and ID*. MK G regarded the market stall as 'straightforward, really good outreach work' and has since followed up the initiative with a two-day audience development project at the Community Desk in the centre of Milton Keynes promoting an exhibition of photographs taken at the Butlins Holiday Camps in the 1960s and 1970s.

Both organisations feel the model 3 initiative was an excellent learning opportunity; the lessons learned continue to inform the education, audience development, data collection and marketing practices of both organisations.

Good practice

- Having two artists working together and jointly leading sessions
- Face-to-face recruitment of young people and seeking their input about the timing and publicising of sessions proved a good way of engaging with people who would not have been reached via more formal networks or school

- The artists' and organisations' flexibility; they found ways to respond to the groups' needs and support the continuation of the project
- Developing a project around 'identity' and using life-size profiles successfully engaged the young people – it offered them safe boundaries but also freedom to express their ideas
- Finishing the work to a high standard and publicly exhibiting the work engendered a feeling of pride amongst participants
- The market stall exhibition enabled MK G to reach people that do not visit the gallery and provided an excellent platform for showing participants' work
- Having experienced artists who recognised the potential severity of the young people's problems and were quick to draw these issues to artworks-mk and MK G's attention
- Bringing in additional staff, one with a social work background, enabled the artists to focus on creative activity

Learning points

- The lessons learned from the project continue to inform the education, audience development and marketing practices of both organisations
- The project emphasised the need for allowing adequate time to plan and research projects and for organisations to clearly identify their own goals and find common ground with partners
- Setting genuine targets can be extremely difficult – there is sometimes a need for a reference point or benchmark outside of the arts
- One of the lessons artworks-mk and MK G feel they have taken from the project is the importance of setting reasonable aims and objectives (more is not necessarily better) and ensuring procedures are in place for measuring whether targets have been met
- Tying in work to a fixed exhibition slot can be problematic – a sufficient amount of time needs to be built in to cover potential planning difficulties and the need to work flexibly and at a pace appropriate for participants
- The importance of implementing procedures for protecting vulnerable groups and the artists working with them
- Work with some groups, such as young people with challenging behaviour, requires a high staff to participant ratio and there can be value in building into a project the expertise of specialists, such as youth workers
- It can take considerable time to build up trust and for people to feel confident about moving from their 'home' environment to an unfamiliar environment
- Intergenerational working needs to be handled sensitively and a longer time frame than planned was needed to achieve such goals
- Drawing in non-arts agencies at an earlier stage would have placed the project on a stronger footing in terms of its continuation and sustainability

Further information

Websites
http://www.artworks-mk.co.uk   artworks-mk
http://www.mk-g.org   MK G

A.1.4 Vita Nova

Summary

Organisation: Bournemouth Theatre in Education (BTiE), Boscombe

Activity: Vita Nova, a theatre company of recovering addicts, worked with Muiruri (from BTiE) and members of Dorset Police to produce *Dream On*, an original adaptation of Shakespeare's *A Midsummer Night's Dream* Director/facilitator: **Sharon Muiruri, BTiE**

Budget: Funding originally came from Bournemouth Borough Council, Boscombe Single Regeneration Budget and Southern Arts

Dates: weekly evening rehearsals took place from March 2002 to September 2002 and there were eight full day rehearsals. *Dream On* was performed on two dates in September 2002 and on three dates in December 2002

Participants: people in recovery from drug and/or alcohol addiction

Arts Council research: interviews with director/facilitator and with eight members of the cast (six from Vita Nova and two from Dorset Police); observation

Outputs:

- the devising and rehearsal period for the September performances comprised 14 weekly evening sessions at Clubhouse and six weekly evening sessions and eight full days at Boscombe Centre for Community Arts (BCCA)
- the *Dream On* cast consisted of 16 members of Vita Nova, two members of Dorset Police and three children of the cast
- approximately 160 people attended the September performances (over two nights) of *Dream On* and 220 people attended the December performances (over three nights)
- Vita Nova currently has 15-20 active members but since the company's formation approximately 80 people have participated in the project

Vita Nova was formed in 1999 when Sharon Muiruri approached a group of people who were in recovery from drug addiction to work with her in devising a drugs education play. The project was originally set up with short term aims (to create a play) but four years on Vita Nova is an independent company and registered charity with two members of staff. Vita Nova delivers a programme of drugs education work and it has devised and performed two plays on a drugs related theme – *Scratchin' the Surface* and *The Mule*.

In 2002, Vita Nova worked with Muiruri to create *Dream On*, an original adaptation of Shakespeare's *A Midsummer Night's Dream*. The play was the group's third piece of community theatre and a departure from their previous plays which had been based on their personal experiences as people recovering from addiction. The cast included members of Vita Nova and two members of Dorset Police. The Arts Council research looked at people's involvement in *Dream On* but also more generally at their longer term involvement in Vita Nova.

Organisations

BTiE is part of Bournemouth Education Directorate's Lifelong Learning Unit and it has two full-time directors and an administrator. The company is based at the Boscombe Centre for Community Arts (BCCA) and its aims include using theatre to raise learners' achievement, inspire literacy, tackle social exclusion and develop personal, social and health education.

Vita Nova was formed in 1999 when one of BTiE's directors, Sharon Muiruri, approached a group of people who were in recovery from drug addiction to work with her in devising a drugs education play. Four years on Vita Nova is an independent company employing two members of staff. The group generally meet one evening a week and more frequently when rehearsing for performances. Participants involved in Vita Nova's drug education programme commit up to three days a week of their time.

Aims and objectives

Muiruri's original aim was to create a good play that could be taken to schools:

> My initial idea was that I wanted a good play that we can take to young people. It would be more authentic and have more clout because these people weren't just talking, they'd been there so could really share from the heart. It wasn't somebody talking who didn't know what they were talking about.
> Director/facilitator

When the group started to rehearse, Muiruri came to realise the work was also therapeutic for the group and complemented the 12-step recovery programme, a programme adapted from the recovery programme of Alcoholics Anonymous. The 12 steps include: admitting to a drug problem; seeking help; self-appraisal; confidential self-disclosure; making amends when possible where harm has been done; and supporting other drug addicts who want to recover. Muiruri subsequently developed the following aims and objectives for Vita Nova:

- to improve the self-esteem of the recovering addicts who participate as members of Vita Nova
- to complement the group's ongoing recovery
- to encourage integration back into society through participation with Vita Nova
- to challenge, through theatre, myths and stereotypes as to what an addict is and how he/she fits into society
- to develop knowledge and understanding of drug addiction through performance and discussion
- to give the audience informed choices about addiction

Dream On was part of the group's programme of work. It sought to build bridges between the police and people in recovery, provide Vita Nova with an opportunity to work from a classic script and, as only one member of the cast had performed Shakespeare before, it was thought it would be a levelling experience for both Vita Nova and the police.

Project planning and management

Having devised and performed two community plays on the subject of drugs, Muiruri felt Vita Nova needed to do something 'a bit cheerful'. She had the idea that it might be fun for Vita Nova and members of the Dorset Police to work together to create an adaptation of Shakespeare's *A Midsummer Night's Dream*. Vita Nova already worked closely with the Dorset Police on drugs education but it was an opportunity to develop relations further and perhaps change some people's perceptions. Over a period of approximately 20 weeks Muiruri worked with the group to create *Dream On*.

Recruitment of participants

Muiruri, when tasked with creating a drugs education play for young people, was keen to involve recovering addicts themselves in telling 'how it is from the street'. She visited a drama group that had been meeting at the Clubhouse, a drop-in centre for recovering drug addicts, to see if any of them would be interested in making a play. 'I was quite direct about it, I said does anybody want to come and make a play?'. Seven people turned up at the BCCA studio the following week and worked with her to create *Scratchin' the Surface*, a play about a young man's journey into drug addiction and the impact this has on his family and friends – the theatre group, Vita Nova, was born. Recruitment is now ongoing – people continue to join from the Clubhouse but also from other recovery centres. All of Vita Nova's members are in recovery and are 'clean'.

To begin with, weekly rehearsals for *Dream On* took place at the Clubhouse – this was a way of attracting new members and taking drama workshops further into the recovering community. Rehearsals later then moved to BCCA. The cast included 15 members of Vita Nova. Muiruri also recruited two officers from Dorset Police – both had been actively involved in the company's education work but neither had done any drama since school. Three of the cast's children were also in the play.

Project activity

Vita Nova's first play, *Scratchin' the Surface*, was created though an intense and emotional process of devising and improvisation.

> There was a lot of catharsis going on and what was interesting was as we acted out the scenes what it was giving to the group, which is what drama

can give, is perspective from all sides. So you weren't seeing yourself... what they were doing was seeing the whole picture.
Director/facilitator

Scratchin' was first performed by the group at BCCA in April 1999 and has since been performed in schools in Bournemouth, Poole and Dorset, as well as in other settings such as rehabilitation centres. Following the play there is a question and answer session where members of the cast answer questions put to them by the audience. The group has also devised and performed *The Mule*, a play which gives a global perspective and insight into drug trafficking and the cost to human life. Vita Nova has developed a drug awareness programme comprising drug education talks, peer education and training sessions for youth workers and others working in the field.

In 2002, Vita Nova worked with Muiruri and two members of the Dorset Police to create their third piece of community theatre, *Dream On*. The play was a departure from their previous plays which have been based on their personal experiences as people recovering from addiction.

The first set of sessions were focused on team building and playing with some of the themes in *A Midsummer Night's Dream*. The focus was to actively include as many people as possible in the play. There was an emphasis on physical theatre, eg the cast became the wood and Titania and Oberon had large groups of attendants. The theme of the 60s was also very much involved right from the start of the process and was evident in the style of music, dress and general atmosphere of the piece.

> I knew from the start that I wanted the play to be physical, earthy and very much engaged with the audience and set in the round. I wanted us to do our own style and not to create an overly romantic version of the play.
> Director/facilitator

Muiruri gradually introduced the script and as the group began to work around particular scenes, she noted 'there was a sense of real achievement and delight as we began to share rough versions of various scenes in the play'. The play took on increasing momentum as it became obvious who should play which character and the group took on the task of trying to learn their lines. *Dream On* was performed for the first time as part of the Boscombe Arts Festival in September 2002.

Outcomes

Eight of the 17 cast members were interviewed about their involvement in the project – six of the interviewees were in recovery so it was appropriate to interview them about the role Vita Nova had played in that process, while two of the interviewees were from Dorset Police.

Increasing confidence and self-esteem
People who have had problems with drugs and alcohol can have low self-esteem, as Muiruri explained. 'If you've got to the point where you've gone to rehab, probably, and it's not true of everybody, but probably you've hit very much a rock bottom. Part of the recovery process involves building up self-esteem'.

All eight cast members said they felt proud of what they as individuals had achieved and what the group as a whole had achieved. Those in recovery cited a whole range of different things that they took pride in: one had been given a certificate – 'it's one of the few things I've ever been given' – one was proud of 'seeing something through to a conclusion', one had auditioned and landed a major role in another drama company's production, three said they were proud of having 'done' Shakespeare, two long-standing members were proud of the company's journey towards independence and several mentioned the importance of the company's education work.

> It's sad no-one ever clapped me for anything in my life [at the end of the play] I got quite emotional. It was nice.
> Participant

> With Shakespeare I was up for it but dubious, sceptical I'd pull it off. A lot of us had never done it before... But doing something as big as Shakespeare – now I've got used to the dialogue I feel we could do anything.
> Participant

The two members of Dorset Police similarly felt proud of their involvement in *Dream On*. One was pleased he had done something he had never done before and thought he could never do, while the other felt he had expanded his comfort zone and had tried (and surprisingly enjoyed) performing a play – something that he had previously hated at school.

Some members of the cast referred to Vita Nova doing 'good' plays, or to having done 'good' performances – achieving something that was perceived as being of good quality by audiences and participants enhanced feelings of achievement.

> ...a lot of those things like self-esteem come out of feeling that you've done something that's good, and strong and works. That gives you confidence. And I feel that is the facilitator's job to ensure that quality and push for it, demand it to a certain extent.
> Director/facilitator

Seven of the eight people interviewed agreed with the statement 'the project has helped me feel good about myself' (one neither agreed or disagreed). A recurring theme was the impact the project had had on their confidence and sense of self-worth.

... I wasn't worth a damn, there was no purpose to my life... a year ago I couldn't have talked to you, I didn't talk to anybody... What has helped me, it helped me build self-esteem and confidence.
Participant

Doing this has helped me be more confident with people. I think I surprised myself, I can do this and I've got something to give people and have the nerve it takes to face people.
Participant

I didn't have a lot of confidence because of the drugs but it [Vita Nova] has brought out natural confidences, it's helping me bring that out.
Participant

The confidence people had developed had also transferred to other areas of their lives; several said they found they could now talk more easily to people in social and other situations and that it had helped them in other circumstances whether it be selling an idea or chairing a meeting.

Providing structure
Vita Nova members are in different stages of recovery; some have been clean for years and are leading relatively stable lives while others are in the early stages of recovery from alcohol and drugs. Individuals referred to addicts' lifestyles as being 'chaotic', 'unmanageable' and 'without rules' – finding a structure is one of the elements required in recovery. As Muiruri explained, 'the time when people have completed their treatment is often a very fragile period when people are at risk of re-entering the world of drug use'.

Vita Nova gets people up and moving in the mornings; its members have to be at specific places at specific times, and those involved in the education work make a three-day a week commitment. Several members referred to the importance of structure to their ongoing recovery and Vita Nova's role in that.

It's part of my recovery in that I'm doing something structured. We're all in the same boat – it's a safe environment. If I've got a problem I can talk to someone.
Participant

It's given me structure – I'm getting up three times a week going into schools. The self-esteem and stuff is important too, that's part of the recovery.
Participant

However, although the project provides structure, Muiruri and Vita Nova also have to be flexible and support the needs of those who are in the very early stages of recovery, who will have meetings to attend (Narcotics Anonymous) and are learning to be committed to something again.

Giving something back
Vita Nova's education work in particular gives recovering addicts a way of 'giving something back' and using their experience in a positive way. As one interviewee put it, 'it gives me a sense that it wasn't all such a waste of time'. One of the 12 steps concerns 'making good' the harm you have caused – participation in Vita Nova's education programme appears to support that particular objective.

> And the work in schools too, I'm proud of that. It gives you a sense of well being that you're doing something useful.
> Participant

> It helps me on a daily basis to remember where I came from because it's easy to forget how bad it was. I'm reiterating how bad it was [through drama and schools work] and that has a positive effect – it's helping people.
> Participant

> ... I could see a good purpose in doing it [*Scratchin'*]. And also, a way of helping my brother live on and maybe help one or two children not go down that way. Kind of a way of turning a negative into a positive.
> Participant

Sense of belonging and support
All eight interviewees felt they had been a member of a team. Individuals had made new 'safe' friends through Vita Nova and the supportive nature of the group was referred to by several members of the group, some referring to it as a family.

> ... I can come in and talk to Sharon [the Director] and the guys – they help people. If I got through a bad patch they help me and I'm not on my own.
> Participant

> I think when you're working to the same objective you forget about your background and anything else because you're all focused. You're all in the same position, you've all got nerves and that makes you quite a solid group, a more emphatic group because you've all got the same problems and the same goals, you all want to do well, you're all nervous but you don't want to let each other down.
> Participant

Muiruri feels that the power of theatre and drama is that it's not just about individuals – it takes a team:

... it's not just about individuals because they are very self-obsessed sometimes. But in a piece of theatre you have to bigger than yourself. You've got to think you could let other people down and that could save your life, if you're thinking shall I have a really depressing day at home today and maybe go out and get some stuff or actually I need to be in rehearsals?
Director/facilitator

All six of those in recovery felt they had got to know people that lived in their area better, all six felt more strongly that they belonged to a community since joining the project and four of them felt more positive about where they lived. All six had made new friends through the project and felt that if the project ended it was very likely they would stay friends with some of them. One the Vita Nova aims is to encourage integration back into society.

Integration is huge! Getting into school situations, talking to people you wouldn't normally find yourself talking to like policemen, the mayor, councillors, people from education.
Director/facilitator

Drama skills and appreciation of the arts
All eight felt they had developed skills through the project; frequently people referred to the development of skills in drama. Some of the cast members had had some involvement in other artforms in the two years before joining Vita Nova, such as music or crafts. However, seven of the eight had had no or very little experience of drama/theatre before Vita Nova and had not done a project like it before, and all felt they had developed a better appreciation of drama. All eight felt the project had broadened their horizons/outlook.

Enjoyment
All those interviewed had enjoyed doing the project 'very much' and all six Vita Nova members were planning on continuing their involvement. Members referred to sessions as 'fun', 'a laugh', 'an escape' and 'relaxing'.

Evaluation

There are two main strands to the evaluation work conducted by Muiruri: ongoing evaluation with schools; and ongoing evaluation of participants and their development.

All teachers, pupils and Vita Nova members are asked to complete evaluation forms after watching *Scratchin'* or GCSE students perform their theatre-in-education pieces. After public performances of *Scratchin'* the audience are asked to write down their spontaneous responses to what they have seen and in schools each pupil has the opportunity to write anonymous questions. Muiruri has also interviewed a sample of pupils some time after seeing the play. More rigorous evaluation exploring the longer term impact of the drugs education work on young people in Bournemouth, Poole and Dorset would require additional resources and research expertise.

Other methods used by Muiruri have included keeping a reflective journal, interviewing individual participants and facilitating group discussions. This work has fed into her MPhil and into written reports that describe the impact of the group and their work (see 2.11 Further information). However, she is aware that her work could be criticised on the grounds of being subjective and is hoping to involve an external evaluator in the future. Muiruri did not evaluate Dream On but a PhD student from Exeter University has since included it in her research.

After the project

Following the first play, *Scratchin'*, Muiruri felt it was vital not to end there. 'I could see how important it was for Vita Nova to continue and to finish at that point could have been detrimental.' She noted that the time between the project ending and beginning again was very difficult for some members of the group. Four years on Vita Nova is an independent company and registered charity. Four of the original seven participants are still involved in the company (two are paid staff). Vita Nova is in a transitional stage where it is becoming an independent organisation. Muiruri, whose role has changed to one of mentor, is supporting them in this process. Dream On then was not so much a self-contained project as part of a continuing programme of work.

Good practice

- Strong partnerships developed with recovery centres and Dorset Police
- The long-running nature of Vita Nova has provided individuals with continuity during their ongoing recovery and supported the development of long-lasting outcomes
- Schools and other audiences have been very positive about Vita Nova's work - this has contributed to members' confidence and self-esteem
- Flexibility to accommodate a diverse group, some of whom are in the very early stages of recovery and others who have been clean for a number of years and living stable lives
- The recruitment of the original members eg visiting the Clubhouse and asking them if they would like to make a play rather than relying on flyers or a written invitation
- Development of a strong sense of ownership among members, in particular, *Scratchin' the Surface* is 'their' play because it dramatises episodes from their lives
- Muiruri providing Vita Nova with continuity, from the project's inception through to its transition to an independent theatre company

- In an area where there is a big drugs problem, Vita Nova has given hope to the recovering population of Boscombe and challenged stereotypes of who an addict is

Learning points

- The devising of the first play, *Scratchin'*, was an emotionally charged process. While the group had a support system, the director did not. Anyone embarking on a similar project should consider building in provision for a counsellor or some other sponsor that they can talk to
- One of the things Muiruri learned early on was how well drama and theatre can support people's ongoing recovery. This was not an original project aim but has since become a core part of Vita Nova's ethos
- After the highs of performance there is inevitably a low. However, those who had engaged in such an intense and emotional creative process as *Scratchin'* possibly felt this more acutely. Arts practitioners involved in a similar process may want to take this on board when handling the closure of projects

Further information

Publications
Muiruri, S. (1999). *Scratchin' the Surface: Drugs Education Project, Report Part 1, Working with a Group of Recovering Addicts.* Bournemouth: Bournemouth Theatre in Education.

Muiruri, S. (1999). *Scratchin' the Surface: Drugs Education Project, Report Part 2, Working with GCSE Groups and Feeder Schools.* Bournemouth: Bournemouth Theatre in Education.

Muiruri, S. (2000) *Scratchin' the Surface: Drugs Education Project, Report Part 3.* Bournemouth: Bournemouth Theatre in Education.

Muiruri, S. (2000). 'Scratchin' the Surface with Vita Nova', *Drama Magazine,* Winter 2000, **8**, 1, 24-30 [Online]
http://www.dramamagazine.co.uk/dm/scratchin.pdf

Websites
http://www.vitanova.co.uk   Vita Nova

Appendix 2: Impacts of the arts identified in reviews and audits

Study and methodology	Impacts
DCMS, 1999 Following the publication of *Bringing Britain together* PAT 10 was established to explore good practice in using arts, sports and leisure to engage people in poor neighbourhoods *Method*: PAT 10, a group of Government officials and experienced practitioners, met four times; subgroups focused on specific issues (good practice, funding, etc); submissions were received from organisations; the PAT visited six arts agencies; research surveys explored existing literature in the arts and in sports. The final report does not contain much in the way of hard evidence; however, it does include some case studies and presents views as to impacts.	A small number of short case studies provided as evidence of the positive contribution arts, sports and leisure can have in areas of health, employment, crime reduction and education. Among the noted impacts are: • economic benefits (increased employment opportunities and equipping individuals with transferable skills) • self-confidence, self-respect and sense of achievement • social, organisational and marketable skills • helping communities express identity • changed perceptions of area • build outside links for insular communities A key finding was the absence of 'hard' evidence of the regenerative impact of arts and sport.
Health Development Agency, 2000 Focus on arts projects aimed at community participation, capacity building and regeneration, as well as those with health or health promotion objective. *Method*: literature review; visits to 15 projects; drawing up of criteria for analysis (a); survey of projects (90/246 responded).	An overwhelming number of projects identified increased sociability (through friendship), self-esteem, personal development, confidence and the improvement of mental health as benefits of participation in arts projects. Evidence was mostly anecdotal – no projects had devised rigorous instruments of measurement. Many projects stated work had informal educational value via development of language, creative and social skills.

Study and methodology	Impacts
	Overall, there was a lack of evidence about direct health benefits but stronger evidence of the role the arts play in improving mental health.
Group for Large Local Authority Museums (GLLAM), 2001 Focuses on social outcomes of museum initiatives that have engaged with people at risk of exclusion or sought to address wider issues of inequality and disadvantage. *Method*: interviews with all 22 GLLAM directors, telephone/face-to-face interviews with 25 project leaders, site visits to 10 museums.	• personal growth and development • community empowerment • the representation of inclusive communities • promoting healthier communities • enhancing educational attainment • tackling unemployment • tackling crime
Bowles, 1991 quoted in Shaw, 1999 Evaluation of a pilot training course involving 17 women in Dublin in which arts activities were used as tools for community action and social change, as well as personal development. Evaluation involved measuring the impact of the course on the individual, group and community.	• reaffirmation of self-worth, skills and creativity • arts, organisational and communication skills • self-confidence • awareness of how collective, creative action can achieve change • awareness of community issues • involvement in community activities • ability to work as a group • spread of arts skills throughout community • community action • increased working within communities • more local control • local identity and cohesion
Williams, 1996 and 1997 Two-year Australian study focused on measuring impact of 95 community-based arts projects. *Method*: nine case studies; survey of	• develops social capital • builds and develops communities • activates social change • develops human capital • improves economic performance

Study and methodology	Impact
198 organisers and 200 observers. Indicators developed to assess the social, artistic, educational and economic benefits of the projects.	
Matarasso, 1997 Comedia study aimed to identify evidence of social impact of arts participation and identify ways of assessing social impact. *Method*: case study research in nine UK locations, Helsinki and New York. Method: project visits, formal interviews and focus group discussion with participants (a) and with artists, observer groups and others (b). Participant questionnaire achieved 513 responses, questions drawn up to form common framework of inquiry for each case study.	• personal development • social cohesion • community empowerment and self-determination • local image and identity • imagination and vision • health and well being
Carpenter, 1999 An evaluation of London Arts Board's 1998/9 Regional Challenge, a funding programme directed at the arts and socially excluded communities. *Method*: analysis of self-evaluations, gathered evidence, and marketing techniques of six projects; four criteria used to develop a common framework for evaluating the quality of participative processes.	• engaged audiences • sustained audience commitment to the work of projects over an extended period
Harland et al, 2000 Three-year study of secondary school arts education in England and Wales. *Method*: questionnaires to 2,000+ Year 11 pupils; interview programme with employers and employees; in-depth interviews with pupils, art teachers, senior school managers; observation of art lessons at five case study schools.	• heightened enjoyment, excitement, fulfilment and therapeutic release of tensions • skills and knowledge associated with artforms • knowledge of social and cultural issues • personal and social development • creativity and thinking skills

Study and methodology	Impact
	• communication and expressive skills
	• some effects transferred to other contexts
	• some effects on school culture and the local community
	• art itself was an outcome

(a) Details are not included in methodology although it is noted that they varied in their formality.

(b) In Batley and Portsmouth only. The idea was developed from Williams' study.

Appendix 3: Template for artist interviews

The template below outlines key themes and questions; it is an interview guide, not a questionnaire. The themes/questions were formally addressed over at least two interviews. There was also variation in detail depending on what issues arose and who was being interviewed. The early interviews focused more heavily on project initiation and planning while the final interview focused more on issues around practice in relation to a particular project, outcomes, evaluation, sustainability, lessons learned etc

1   Planning

Factors considered in planning: What considered (finances, availability of artists, recruitment of artists/participants, partners, timing). How were participants recruited? Were participants involved in planning the project or consulted before the project? How important is this?

Considerations working with group: Were there any considerations working with group that you might not consider with others? eg practical considerations, food, transportation, structure of day/workshops, variety/concentration, pace of progress, subject matter etc

Aims and objectives: Does the project have aims and objectives? Is it important to have them? Why? How were aims and objectives set (with participants, 'partners')? To what extent do you reflect back on aims and objectives during the project? Have they changed over the course of the work? Did you discuss aims and objectives with participants (including social objectives like 'increase confidence')? Why/why not?

Partnerships: Aside from participants, who have you considered to be 'partners' in the project? What is their role? How are these partnerships working – what's been good/not so good about them? How could they have been more effective?

2   Working approach

Can you tell me about your approach to working with groups? Are there any values or principles that underpin your work (formal/informal)? What sort of qualities does an artist working in this area need?

What sort of environment/atmosphere do you try to create?

How would you describe your role? To what extent are you directing what happens and to what extent is the work participant-led?

3 Working with participants

Can you tell me how you described the project to participants in the early stages – to what extent are they prepared for what's going to happen? How have you gone about getting individuals interested in the early stages? What sort of reception did you get?

Some of the good practice literature talks about identifying needs of participants and responding to that. I wondered how you feel about that in relation to your project?

To what extent is each session structured/planned and to what extent open? What about the overall programme of work? To what extent do you need to cater for individual needs?

4 Nature of participation

How many sessions? How many weeks? How many participants (max/min/core)? Content of sessions and nature of work? Any thoughts about: level of intensity; challenge/risk taking or safe/comfortable; relevance/draw on own experiences/background?

5 Pride in achievement

Does 'quality' or 'excellence' have any bearing on your work? In what way (process, materials, standard of practice)? What do terms mean? Does quality of final product matter or is it about process? Any relationship between pride in quality of achievement and outcome?

6 Exit strategy and sustainability

When planning this project did you consider an 'exit strategy' at all (eg what happens next, future progression for those who might be interested)? Are there any issues about sustainability you'd like to mention?

Do you think the project will have a long-term legacy on yourselves or the organisation eg profile raising, practice, incorporation of lessons learned? In what way/s?

7   Evaluation

What sort of outcomes are you hoping to achieve? Has any evaluation been planned? Are you yourselves intending to evaluate the project? How do you intend to do this? (Who involved? How involved? At what stage?)

Appendix 4: Participant questionnaire

How did it go?
*(Double-check person hasn't filled in baseline. Explain purpose of survey. Ask all questions marked *)*

Project:

What did you think of the project?

*1. Can you tell me how you came to be doing the project? *No prompt. Tick most appropriate box.*

☐ Heard about project and wanted to take part *(heard about project where?_____)*
☐ Was accompanying a friend/taken along to project by a friend
☐ Member of (organised) group the project was visiting
☐ Other *(please describe)*_____

*2. Have you been involved in a project like this before?

☐ Yes   ☐ No   ☐ Don't know

3. I'd now like you to think back to when you first got involved in the project. I'm going to read out a list of words that might describe how you felt and I'd like you tell me which apply to you. *(Showcard A)*

☐ Suspicious	☐ Disinterested	☐ Excited	☐ Negative	☐ Relaxed	☐ Scared/fright.
☐ Hostile	☐ Confident	☐ Positive	☐ Proud	☐ Satisfied	☐ A bit nervous
☐ Cool	☐ Inspired	☐ Interested	☐ Optimistic	☐ Other_____	

4. I'd now like you to think about how you're feeling now at/close to the end of the project. I'm going to read out the same list of words and I'd like you tell me which words apply to you now. *(Showcard 4)*

☐ Suspicious	☐ Disinterested	☐ Excited	☐ Negative	☐ Relaxed	☐ Scared/fright.
☐ Useless	☐ Confident	☐ Positive	☐ Proud	☐ Satisfied	☐ A bit nervous
☐ Cool	☐ Inspired	☐ Interested	☐ Optimistic	☐ Other_____	

* 5. How much have you enjoyed doing the project?

☐ Very much   ☐ Some   ☐ No feelings either way   ☐ Not very much   ☐ Not at all

* 6. Would you like to be involved in more projects like this one?

☐ Yes   ☐ No   ☐ Not sure

147

* 7. I'd now like to find out whether you think you had a say over what happened in the project. I'm going to read out a list of statements, please tell me whether you agree or disagree with each choosing your answer from this card. *(Showcard B)*

During the project...	Agree	Neither agree or disagree	Disagree
(a) ... I had freedom to use and develop my own ideas	☐	☐	☐
(b) ... the artists didn't seem interested in what I thought	☐	☐	☐
(c) ... I didn't have much of a say over what happened	☐	☐	☐
(d) ... I sometimes felt challenged (in a good way) to try new things or think in a different way	☐	☐	☐
(e) ... I got help and support when I needed it	☐	☐	☐

8. Is there anything more you'd like to say about the way the sessions were run?
(Prompt: any things that they particularly liked or didn't like? would they do anything differently?)

You and the arts

*9. Can you tell me how much experience you had of [artform] before this project?
(As attender or participant)

☐ Lots   ☐ A fair amount   ☐ A little   ☐ None

Comments....

*10. How much did you have to do with the arts in general before the project?

☐ Lots   ☐ A fair amount   ☐ A little   ☐ Nothing

Comments....

*11. Do you feel your views about the arts have changed as a result of being involved in the project?

☐ Yes, a lot   ☐ Yes, a little   ☐ No *(Go to Q13)*

*12. How are your views different from the ones you had before?

What did you gain from the project?

*13a. Do you think you made any new friends through the project? If yes, how many

☐ None   (Q14) ☐ 1-2   ☐ 3-5   ☐ 6-10   ☐ 11-20   ☐ 20+

13b. Is it likely you'll stay friends with any of them once the project finishes?

☐ Very likely   ☐ Fairly likely   ☐ I'd like to but not sure/maybe ☐ Not very likely

*14. Has being involved in the project changed the way you think about yourself and what you can do? *(Prompt: any effect on confidence or self-esteem?)*

*15. Do you think you developed any new skills through the project?

☐ Lots   ☐ Some   ☐ None   ☐ Don't know

*16. I'm going to read you out some statements and I'd like you to tell me if you agree of disagree with each. *(Showcard C) Only ask if they feel they got better at items if answer is agree.*

During the project I …	Agree	Neither agree or disagree	Disagree
* (a) Was creative and used my imagination	☐	☐	☐
(b) Gained experience in computers/new technology	☐	☐	☐
*(c) Completed tasks/saw things through to end	☐	☐	☐
*(d) Thought problems through and came up with some answers/solutions	☐	☐	☐
* (e) Worked with others as part of a team	☐	☐	☐
* (f) Listened to what others in the team had to say	☐	☐	☐
* (g) Put across my thoughts, opinions and ideas	☐	☐	☐
(h) Worked with numbers	☐	☐	☐

*17a. Do you feel proud of what you personally achieved on the project?

☐ Yes   ☐ Not really *(Go to Q19)*   ☐ Don't know *(Go to Q18)*

*17b. Can you tell me a bit more about that? *(How do you feel? What are you proud of?)*

18. Do you feel proud of what the group as a whole achieved?

☐ Yes   ☐ Not really ☐ Don't know

*19a. Now thinking about your involvement in the project can you tell me how much do you agree or disagree with the following statements?

                                                 Agree   Neither   Disagree

Being involved in this project...

agree of disagree

* (a) ... has helped me appreciate [artform] more
* (b) ... has helped me feel good about myself
* (c) ... has helped me express myself
* (d) ... has broadened my horizons/outlook
* (e) ... has improved my quality/enjoyment of life more generally

*19b. And again, would you agree or disagree?

During the project I...	Agree	Neither agree or disagree	Disagree
(h) ... enjoyed talking with someone new from a different generation or different ethnic culture from me	☐	☐	☐
(i) ... learned more about people from different generations or ethnic cultures	☐	☐	☐
* (j) ... generally felt better/healthier (*either physically or mentally*)	☐	☐	☐
(* k) ... felt I had more energy/motivation	☐	☐	☐
(l) ... got to know people who live in my area better	☐	☐	☐
(m) ... felt more positive about where I live	☐	☐	☐
(n) ... felt more strongly that I belonged to a community	☐	☐	☐

20a. Are you planning on doing any of the following things in the next 12 months?
(*If yes, ask if they would 'like to' do it, are definitely planning do to it or have already taken steps ie joined a course/training scheme*)

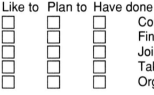

Like to Plan to Have done
☐ ☐ ☐ Continue some kind of involvement in [artform]
☐ ☐ ☐ Find a job/new job
☐ ☐ ☐ Join training scheme
☐ ☐ ☐ Take a course
☐ ☐ ☐ Organise a community, voluntary or arts project

20b. Did doing the project play any part in that decision?

21. Is there anything else you'd like to tell me about your time on the project?

Some background information about yourself

23.

*a) Sex: Female   ☐ Male

150

*b) Age:

15 or under	16-17	18-20	21-24	25-54	55+
☐	☐	☐	☐	☐	☐

c) Which of the following best describes your ethnic background?

☐ White   ☐ Black Caribbean   ☐ Indian
☐ Chinese   ☐ Black African   ☐ Pakistani
☐ Other   ☐ Black British   ☐ Bangladeshi
                     ☐ Black other   ☐ Asian other

d) What do you normally do during weekdays?

☐ At school (pre 16)   ☐ In full-time education (post 16)   ☐ Full-time employed
☐ Part-time employed   ☐ Employment/training scheme ☐ Unemployed/looking for work
☐ Retired   ☐ Other

FOR POST-16 INTERVIEWEES

e) Highest level educational qualifications?

☐ No qualifications   ☐ GCSE passes   ☐ GCSE above C
☐ A levels   ☐ Degree or above   ☐ Other NVQ, HND, BTEC etc

Thanks for your help.

References

Addressing social exclusion: a framework for action (1999). London: Arts Council of England.

Allin, P. (2000). *Creative Research – A Modernising Government Review of DCMS's Statistical & Social Policy Research Needs*. London: Statistics and Social Policy Unit, Department for Culture, Media and Sport.

Angus, J. (2002). *A Review of Evaluation in Community-based Art for Health Activity in the UK*. London: Health Development Agency.

Arnstein, S. (1971). 'A ladder of citizen participation in the USA', *Journal of the American Planning Association*. Cited in Russell, J. (1998), *Involving users in Evaluation: Discussion Paper 4*. London: Charities Evaluation Services.

Art for Health: a review of good practice in community-based arts projects and initiatives which impact on health and well-being (2000). London: Health Development Agency.

Arts and Sport, Policy Action Team 10: A Report to the Social Inclusion Unit (1999). London: Department of Culture, Media and Sport.

Belfiore, E. (2002). 'Art as a means of alleviating social exclusion: does it really work? A critique of instrumental cultural policies and social impact studies in the UK', *International Journal of Cultural Policy*, **8**, 1, 91-106.

Blake Stevenson Ltd. (2000). *The Role of the Arts in Regeneration*. Edinburgh: Scottish Executive Central Research Unit.

Bringing Britain Together: A National Strategy for Neighbourhood Renewal (1998). London: Cabinet Office.

Carpenter, E. (1999). *The Arts and Inclusion: Evaluation of London Arts Board's 1998/99 Regional Challenge*. London: London Arts Board.

Coalter, F. (2001). *Realising the Potential of Cultural Services: Making a Difference to Quality of Life*. London: Local Government Association.

Count Me In – The Dimensions of Social Inclusion through Culture and Sport (2002). Leeds: Leeds Metropolitan University.

Dewson, S., Eccles, J., Tackey, N. D. & Jackson, A. (2000). *Measuring Soft Outcomes and Distance Travelled: A Review of Current Practice, Research Report No 219*. London: Department for Education and Employment

Glass, N. (2000). *Social Exclusion: concepts, measurement and policy.* Paper delivered at the seventh annual Cathie Marsh Memorial Seminar jointly hosted by the Royal Statistical Society and Social Research Association, 2000.

Hall, R. (2002). 'Tailor-made practice' in Raney (ed) *Engage,* Issue 11: Inclusion Under Pressure. London and Manchester: Engage and Cornerhouse.

Harland, J., Kinder, K., Lord, P., Slott, A., Schagen, I. & Haynes, J. (2000). *The Effects and Effectiveness of Arts Education in School.* Slough: NFER.

Jermyn, H. (2001). *The Arts and Social Exclusion: a review prepared for the Arts Council of England.* [Online] http://www.artscouncil.org.uk [6 September 2003].

Jermyn, H., Bedell, S. & Joy, A. (2000). *New Audiences Programme: Report on the first year 1998-1999.* London: Arts Council of England, unpublished.

Keeping arts safe: protection of children, young people and vulnerable adults in arts activities (2003). London: Arts Council England in collaboration with the NSPCC.

Kleinman, M (1998). *Include Me Out? Case paper 11.* London: Centre for Analysis of Social Exclusion, London School of Economics. Cited in Merli, 2002.

Landry, L., Greene, L., Matarasso, F. & Bianchini, F. (1996). *The Art of Regeneration: Urban renewal through cultural activity.* Stroud: Comedia.

Matarasso, F. (1996). *Defining Values: Evaluating Arts Programmes, The Social Impact of the Arts, Working Paper 1.* Stroud: Comedia.

Matarasso, F. (1997). *Use or Ornament? The Social Impact of Participation in the Arts.* Stroud: Comedia.

Matarasso, F. (1999). *Towards a Cultural Index: Measuring the Cultural Vitality of Communities.* Stroud: Comedia.

Merli, P. (2002). 'Evaluating the social impact of participation in arts activities', *International Journal of Cultural Policy*, **8**, 1, 107-118.

Miles, Dr. A. & McLewin, A. [eds]. (2004). *Doing the Arts Justice: A Literature Review of Arts Practice in the Criminal Justice System.* Canterbury: Unit for the Arts and Offenders.

Moriarty, G. (1998). *Hidden Assets: The Role of Arts in Regeneration.* Bolton: Bolton Libraries Arts and Archives.

Moriarty, G. (2000). *Sharing practice: a guide to self-evaluation for artists, arts organisations and funders working in the context of social exclusion.* [Online] www.newaudiences.org.uk/static/news_story_20030701_4.html [29 January 2004].

Museums and Social Inclusion: The GLLAM Report (2000). Leicester: Research Centre for Museums and Galleries, University of Leicester.

Reeves, M. (2002). *Measuring the Economic and Social Impact of the Arts.* London: Arts Council of England.

Shaw, P. (1999). *The Arts and Neighbourhood Renewal: a literature review to inform the work of Policy Action Team 10,* unpublished.

Shaw, P. (2003). *Social Inclusion/Social Exclusion and Arts Council England – Current Action, Thinking and Recommendations*, unpublished.

Social Exclusion: A response to Policy Action Team 10 from the Arts Council of England (2000). London: Arts Council of England.

Social Inclusion and Community Development Practice (2001). London: Community Development Foundation. [Online] http://www.cdf.org.uk/html.socinc.html [6 June 2001].

Williams, D. (1996). *Creating Social Capital.* Adelaide: Community Arts Network of South Australia. Cited in Williams, D. (1997).

Williams, D. (1997). *How the Arts Measure Up: Australian Research into the Social Impact of the Arts, The Social Impact of the Arts, Working Paper 8.* Stroud: Comedia.

Woolf, F. (1999). *Partnerships for Learning: A Guide to Evaluating Arts Education Projects.* England: Arts Council of England and Regional Arts Boards.